Mike Willesee was born in Perth in 1942. He got his start as a journalist at Perth's *Daily News* before moving to the Melbourne *Age* in 1963. Mike joined Australia's first nightly prime-time current affairs show, *This Day Tonight*, before hosting the ABC's *Four Corners*. In between, he reported the Vietnam War from 1967 to 1971.

Mike created and presented *A Current Affair* for the Nine network (1971–73), then hosted *The Mike Willesee Show* and *Willesee at 7* for Channels 10 and 7. In the '80s, he drew record ratings for his documentaries *Quentin* and *The Hunting Party*, while pioneering FM radio with the 2Day FM licence.

In 1988, Mike led a consortium to save the Sydney Swans, and then served as president until 1993. He then went on to make the documentary films *The Last Warriors* and *Signs From God*, the latter drawing 28 million viewers in the United States. In 2012, a decade after being inducted into the Logie Hall of Fame, Mike joined Channel 7's *Sunday Night* and reclaimed his place as Australia's pre-eminent interviewer.

Mike Willesee, the voice of Australian television for decades, was diagnosed with throat cancer in 2016. In 2017, he released his autobiography, *Memoirs*. He passed away in early 2019.

Also by Mike Willesee

Memoirs

A Sceptic's Search for Meaning

A SPIRITUAL JOURNEY

MIKE WILLESEE

Pan Macmillan Australia

First published 2019 in Macmillan by Pan Macmillan Australia Pty Ltd
1 Market Street, Sydney, New South Wales, Australia, 2000

Copyright © Mike Willesee 2019

The moral right of the author to be identified as the author of this work has been asserted.

All rights reserved. No part of this book may be reproduced or transmitted by any person or entity (including Google, Amazon or similar organisations), in any form or by any means, electronic or mechanical, including photocopying, recording, scanning or by any information storage and retrieval system, without prior permission in writing from the publisher.

Cataloguing-in-Publication entry is available
from the National Library of Australia
http://catalogue.nla.gov.au

Typeset in 12.5/16 pt Bembo by Post Pre-press Group, Brisbane
Printed by McPherson's Printing Group

Excerpts, research and material from the books *Reason to Believe* and *Unseen: New Evidence* used with kind permission from Ron Tesoriero, all rights reserved.

Transcript from videotaped component of 'Signs From God' used with kind permission from Trans Media Group, all rights reserved. Transcript from live broadcast component of 'Signs From God' used with kind permission from Fox Broadcasting Company, all rights reserved.

Transcript from 'The Blood of Christ' on *Sunday Night* used with kind permission from the Seven Network, all rights reserved.

The author and the publisher have made every effort to contact copyright holders for material used in this book. Any person or organisation that may have been overlooked should contact the publisher.

Aboriginal and Torres Strait Islander people should be aware that this book may contain images or names of people now deceased.

The paper in this book is FSC® certified. FSC® promotes environmentally responsible, socially beneficial and economically viable management of the world's forests.

Contents

Foreword by Father Mark Withoos — vii

Part One — **A Boy and his God** — 1
One — Born into the Light — 3
Two — Knowing Right from Wrong — 5
Three — A Formative Experience — 9
Four — Turning Away — 15

Part Two — **The Making of a Sceptic** — 19
Five — A New Religion — 21
Six — A Sceptic is Born — 27
Seven — A Chance Meeting — 37

Part Three — **Seeds of Doubt** — 43
Eight — The Premonition and the Prayer — 45
Nine — A Favour for a Friend — 61
Ten — Is Seeing Believing? — 69
Eleven — Evidence — 80

Part Four — **Finding the Story** — 87
Twelve — A Second Chance — 89
Thirteen — The Start of Something — 99
Fourteen — Katya's Story — 107
Fifteen — What to Believe — 126

Part Five — **Signs from God** — 137
Sixteen — Following the Trail — 139
Seventeen — Testing Faith — 148
Eighteen — Bearing Witness — 159
Nineteen — Showing the World — 171

Part Six	The Journey Continues	187
Twenty	What Next?	189
Twenty-one	Things Science Can't Explain	195
Twenty-two	Opening my Heart	205

Part Seven	Continuing the Work	209
Twenty-three	The Host	211
Twenty-four	Jesus' Command	215
Twenty-five	Seeing Clearly	223
Twenty-six	Sacred Heart	228
Twenty-seven	The Blood of Christ	238
Twenty-eight	Convincing Australia	248

Part Eight	A New Phase	257
Twenty-nine	Unfinished Business	259

Afterword by Father Mark Withoos   274

Foreword

Edited extract from the eulogy for Mike Willesee by Father Mark Withoos

Why would a man with Mike Willesee's stellar career and reputation as one of Australia's best journalists dedicate so much of his final years to telling the world about God? And why would he keep doing it, when greeted only with criticism and disbelief?

Let's listen to what Mike himself said in his last interview:

> I think God and religion are just so politically incorrect at the moment. Nobody wants to know. You can be laughed at just for saying you believe in God . . . The work I'm doing now has been difficult. I'm constantly reminded that most journalists would say this is ridiculous. But I've stuck with this story and I'm making progress. It shows the truth of God in the Eucharist. The truth that God is alive in our world and that His hand moves.

The truth that God is alive in our world and that His hand moves.

Mike Willesee saw telling this story to a sceptical world as the most important work he had done. It wasn't about convincing everyone – with Mike it was always about getting to the bottom of things.

Kerry O'Brien said that Mike had an instinct for asking the right question, even if it seemed strange. The question he ultimately came to ask remains the right question, perhaps the best and most fundamental question, for all of us: 'What is this all about?'

In Mike's own words: 'This story is the only one that matters because it's the biggest question that we ask ourselves or deny ourselves but know it's there somewhere. And that is, "What's it all about? Why are we here?"'

It's a basic question and it is the question that Mike, no longer with us, still wants to ask you.

Mike's work is still not complete. He began with his *Memoirs* – what a cracking read they were! After reading the book, I spoke to Mike and said, 'I loved the book, Mike, you're a great storyteller. But there were quite a few expletives in there!' I was having a dig at him.

And he responded, 'Ah, yes, Father, but that's my secular life before God got hold of me. My next book will be the real book – my road to Damascus.'

Cue characteristic Mike Willesee meaningful pause . . .

Part One

A Boy and his God

One

Born into the Light

1942. My father knelt before the altar and, with me in his hands, stretched out his arms so the shard of light streaming through the window of the hospital chapel fell upon me. It was an offering to God.

'I give my son to you,' he said. 'Michael is yours for eternity.'

There was only silence in the chapel.

'But first,' my father pleaded, 'give him back to me.'

I was a newborn but could not hold down any milk. I was skeletal and starving. Mum and Dad had been told to prepare themselves for the worst. Every night, my parents feared I wouldn't make the dawn. In the mornings, when I was still there, Mum fed me incessantly, praying some of the milk might stay down. On this went for almost a week, with my condition worsening – and my parents' distress mounting.

Just when all seemed lost, a new man on the ward – an English doctor – quietly approached them.

'I have heard about your son and I have a particular interest. There is a theory I've been working on and if you allow me to try it on your little boy, then I believe I may be able to save him.'

'Do it,' was Dad's instant reply.

The surgery to open a narrowed valve from my stomach to the small intestine was successful. Later that same week, the English doctor who had saved my life left Perth aboard a ship and returned to England, passing through my parents' life and mine in a most fortunate piece of timing.

I didn't hear this story of my dad's deal with God in full until early 2018, a few months after my autobiography, *Memoirs*, was published. It was told to me then by a mutual friend of my father's and mine, Charles Morton, a lawyer from The Rock, near Wagga Wagga. I was shocked.

Trying to visualise my father in that scene in the hospital chapel was difficult. All his life we saw only glimpses of his own personal emotions. In repressing uncomfortable memories, my father was a master. In being expressive about his personal feelings, he was a miser.

'Charles,' I said. 'This story is so hard for me to believe.'

'Mike, your father was crying as he told it to me,' replied Charles.

Crying was something else my father never did. Despite my ignorance of the deal, it must have seemed to Dad that God had accepted his offer. I faced death three more times as a youngster – when suffering from scarlet fever as a toddler, again at three years of age when I fell into a fire, and then when I got hit by a car that put a hole in the back of my skull at the age of about eight. Each time I survived.

Whenever death drew me in close to its darkness, I found my way back into the light.

Two

Knowing Right from Wrong

My favourite place for family holidays as a kid was Safety Bay.

It was a loose collection of ramshackle shacks set into the dunes and on the headlands just south of Perth. Dad told me the shacks were illegal, that people hadn't sought council approval, they'd just stuck struts in the sand and set up these primitive holiday homes out of old tin and stray lumber. A compound of itinerant families moved in every summer and during school breaks. Technically it was squatting, but if you built one you could rent it out and get a few bob for it and everyone was happy.

Me most of all. Safety Bay was the most magical place in the world to me. The water was crystal clear and full of darting, shimmering fish. The sun was always shining, and birds carolled and squawked from the trees. People at Safety Bay always smiled and laughed. Families had fun and shared what they had.

Dad was a postal worker and union organiser. He had his sights set on a career in politics, but back then we were as staunchly working class as the rest of the families there.

Mum was busy with three kids under the age of seven, from Colleen, the eldest, down to Terry, three, the youngest, with me in the middle. The fourth, Geraldine, was probably on the way, while Don and Peter were still to come. But while Mum might have been a bit tied down with all that, I was six years old and at Safety Bay, I could do anything I wanted. It was total freedom.

There were always other kids around who you could get up to mischief with. Sometimes we'd pinch a box of matches and go off somewhere quiet where no-one was around and light up a patch of the grassy, weedy stuff called Guildford grass. It would go up fast, the little purple flowers would shrivel into cinders in a heartbeat and the seeds would pop and crackle and explode. The whole plant would give off a sweet onion aroma as it burned. To me, it was the smell of freedom.

Whenever I lit the match, I'd dare myself to see how high the flames could get and how far the fire could spread before I lost my bottle and put it out with fistfuls of sand. It was a silly thing to do, but at the time it was like a fight against myself. I was drawn to the danger and loved the smell.

I was wandering around Safety Bay one day feeling that happiness a six-year-old feels, the happiness that exists without needing a reason, when I heard someone raise the alarm: 'Fire!'

People came running from everywhere. Many carried the large hessian bags that people in the compound would attach to their shacks to provide shade and keep the worst of the wind and rain out, the kind you'd pack wheat into.

There was only one source of fresh water in the compound: a pump that needed constant priming. In other words, you needed water in the pump to get water from the pump. With everyone running around screaming, 'Fire! Fire! Fire!' and looking for their loved ones through a pall of smoke that was getting thicker by the minute, the pump needed to be the eye in this hurricane of activity.

A great big man grabbed me and asked, 'Can you prime the pump?'

I didn't have time to think.

'Yes,' I squeaked.

He looked me dead in the eye and said: 'Are you sure? Because once you prime it, you've got to pump it and then you've got to keep pumping it. There'll be no time to waste. Even if nobody wants any water, you need to keep pumping so it's there when we need it.' He looked at me fixedly, asking for as solemn an oath as a six-year-old boy could muster: 'Got that, little man?'

I nodded.

So, I started pumping. And I kept pumping.

All around me was chaos. Smoke was swirling from all directions and stinging my eyes, but I didn't stop. I'd hear people yelling, 'Quick, quick, number six is going up' and 'Help, help, it's getting close to cabin 12'. And even though I felt like my arm was about to fall off, on I pumped.

Finally, after what seemed like forever, the fire was put out and somebody appeared with beer, as often happened in those days. As the beers went around, people gathered, and speeches started up. The feeling of camaraderie among us was fantastic. Even as a kid, I knew I was in the middle of something special. People were exhausted and dirty, with smudges across their faces and burns on their hands and feet, but there was a good feeling in the air. This was our place. These were our people.

The big man who'd asked me to do the pumping had led the firefight. He stepped up for the speech. He talked about how out of adversity we'd found unity. We'd come together to help each other and save the people and the place that we loved.

'This is the Australia we're proud of,' he said.

Then he looked my way. 'But special praise and applause should go to this little bloke standing here.' I could feel people turning and craning to look at me. 'I dunno how his arm is still attached to his shoulder. He's been pumping all afternoon, even when we didn't need it, he never stopped. I told him to keep going and he did. Without him, we could've lost this place.'

People cheered and clapped. And I looked down, blushing beneath my sunburn, embarrassed.

After all, I'd lit the fire.

And I remember thinking: *is this what they call a sin?*

Three

A Formative Experience

As a boy I don't remember anyone ever telling me explicitly that I was going to be a priest. But all my young life, I knew. It was just going to be.

Even before I knew anything of my father offering me to God as a dying baby, I just knew the priesthood was my destiny.

When I wasn't starting fires at Safety Bay, I was mostly an obedient child and on the odd occasion when I broke the rules, I mostly owned up to it. From a young age, I was an altar boy and never missed a Sunday Mass. I voluntarily went to weekday Masses too. I continued this practice throughout primary school and into high school. It wasn't like I shunned all those other things like footy and cricket and mucking around down at the creek but going to Mass made me feel good. Being close to God made me feel good. You're taught that the little white piece of bread is the flesh and blood of Christ. I believed that. It felt good to believe that. And it felt right that pursuing this was my destiny.

Whenever a priest would visit our Christian Brothers school, he'd invariably ask if any boy wanted to be a priest.

I would shoot my hand up and wait for a pat on the head. I wasn't currying favour. I meant it. And, because it was my destiny, I even studied Latin to be closer to God. My experience of school and the Church up to that time was idyllic. It did not prepare me for what was up ahead.

When I was 10 years old, Dad drove me to Bindoon Boys Home and dumped me there. Bindoon was about 100 kilometres north of Perth. It was allegedly an orphanage run by the Christian Brothers, but the world would learn many years later that it was in fact an epicentre of evil for a lost generation of kids who'd been separated from their families in England, Malta and Wales. A home for kids who had been told their parents were dead when they weren't.

These were boys with names and histories and families. They belonged back in their homelands. But all that got erased at Bindoon. Instead of the 'sunshine and oranges' they'd been promised in far-off Australia, they found themselves in a living hell.

Dad, on the other hand, thought that Bindoon was marvellous. He often said that Bindoon's founder, Brother Paul Francis Keaney, was a wonderful man. For years he'd been telling me stories of how Keaney had gone out into the bush to an abandoned farm with these orphans and built a haven – three-storey buildings of classrooms, dormitories and kitchens with Spanish mission designs. Dad would go on and on. Brother Keaney is a great man, he would say.

While I was being driven there, I asked my father, 'Why do I need to go to Bindoon?'

'I want you to toughen up,' was his reply.

I toughened up all right.

Bindoon, as it turned out, was not exactly what my dad had pictured. While he was enjoying a beer with Brother Keaney,

A Boy and his God

I was met by the welcoming committee of boys who were all about my height. They asked me how old I was and when I told them I was ten, they didn't believe me. These slum-born kids were all a few years older than me, and a whole lot tougher.

'Liar!' they shouted. And that's how the first bashing began.

In my first week there, I was bashed unconscious several times by other boys. They didn't need a reason. It was like I was their sport. On one occasion, I woke up not knowing where I was, how I'd got there and what had happened. None of the Brothers were there to help me, it was only later that I realised that they were never seen. It was only the kids I ever saw. These boys were abandoned and now they were enslaved, but free to create their own hierarchies. Within that structure, there was a subgroup of boys with shaved heads who were forbidden to speak to each other. They just loped around the grounds of Bindoon like zombies.

I asked one of the other orphans, 'Why are those boys' heads shaven?'

'I dunno,' said the kid, 'maybe they've got lice.'

'Then why don't you have lice?'

He shrugged.

It was a mystery that stuck in my mind. Even then I knew these shaven-headed kids had copped it. They were the definition of lost souls.

The one bright spot in the Bindoon experience was that I was given the job of assistant rabbit trapper. The chief rabbit trapper was a quiet 16-year-old Welsh boy, and the two of us had to go out each morning to shoot and skin 40 rabbits. It was the only time of the day I enjoyed. The Welsh boy was very sensible and taught me how to dig rabbits up, find their holes, set the traps. I used to practise loading and unloading the gun until I was quick at it. The two of us would time each other killing and skinning a rabbit. Nine seconds is my memory of what we got it down to. I was so proud. I'd never had any bush skills, never had a life like this. I could have done it all day. But unfortunately, I had to go back and join the mob after breakfast.

The other upside of the job was that it gave me access to a gun. Around the end of the first week, I was approached by a gang of bullies who asked me if I could take them out shooting since I had the gun, and, crucially, money to buy bullets. They'd twice tricked me into trusting them before and both times it had ended up with me being bashed or humiliated, but I'd wised up by this time.

I didn't know how to say no – they would have just bashed me there and then – but I wasn't going to be fooled again.

'Yeah, okay,' I said.

I went and got the gun, then headed to the canteen and bought a box of .22-calibre bullets. I had the gun in one hand, my other hand in my pocket playing with the loose bullets as this gang of five and I headed into the bush.

The further we walked, the more nervous I got. I didn't know what they were up to, and I didn't trust my sense of direction to find my way back. I had to take charge.

'This looks good here,' I said. 'Lots of burrows.'

The leader of the pack pushed his chest out: 'Righto, give me the rifle. I'm gunna have first shot.'

I took a breath. 'No, you're not,' I said pointing the gun at him. I was scared, but I'd had enough.

'You're fucken kidding,' he said.

Just like I'd seen at the movies, I aimed the gun down in front of his feet and fired.

'I'm having the first shot,' I said as he leapt back.

I trained the rifle on each of them. 'Have you got the message?' I asked.

In that moment, I had the anger, the pain and the motivation to pull the trigger.

The lot of them suddenly took off, taking refuge behind nearby trees. I put my hand in my pocket to grab another bullet, reloaded and fired at the first tree.

'Billy!' Bang.

Picked out another bullet, reloaded and fired at the next tree: 'Jack!' Bang.

Pulled out another bullet, and did the same again, taking a shot at each of them in turn as I called out their names.

When I was finished, I yelled: 'It's my rifle and I decide who's shooting!'

They obviously got the message because they all bolted back to the orphanage. And they never came near me again.

Dad was right about something. I had toughened up.

A Royal Commission later found that Brother Keaney was one of the worst architects of child abuse in Australia. Far from the saint of Dad's imagination, he was, in fact, a sadistic deviant who governed with violence, fear and savagery. The orphanages Keaney built out in the bush had been constructed by bare-footed boys forced to work with picks and shovels, mixing concrete by hand, in the blazing West Australian heat. Those who couldn't or wouldn't submit to the labour were bashed and flogged. Or worse.

Bindoon was also home to an active paedophile ring to which Keaney turned a blind eye. My sister told me that when Dad found out about all this in his later years, she'd never seen him so upset. And when I heard about it, it made me wonder about exactly what those poor shaven-head boys had endured.

While preparing this book and reflecting on my Bindoon

experience, I had a dream that was so real it could only be described as a flashback.

It took me straight back there. I was standing outside the Bindoon dormitory where I'd been going to bed every night and lying awake shit-scared and terrified. It was morning and we were being ordered to the ablutions block to wash and toilet and so on.

There was a Brother barking orders. I'd never seen him before, but he was an evil-looking man. I was only 10 years old, but I knew instinctively that this was a bad man – not just bad, but evil. This Brother turned his gaze on me, and his eyes bulged and his face turned dark and ugly. Then he came at me, running, crazed and manic, with a fist raised.

Although I was dreaming, I know that it was real – that this was in fact a memory of a real event that I had somehow put out of my mind. In the dream and in my memory, I knew for certain that this Brother hated me and was running at me to beat the living daylights out of me, or worse. As this Bindoon Brother came at me, I knew I was in serious danger and I took off. I ran and hid, ran and hid, ran and hid. And he never caught me.

I woke up from the dream knowing I'd seen evil. And it was real. Can I prove it? No. But do I believe it? Absolutely. Bindoon was not a house of God. It was hell, a Devil's playground. And this Brother was, for me, the Devil himself.

At my birth, my father had brought me into the light and offered me to God, and by the time I was 10, he had unwittingly done the opposite: he had thrust me into the darkness. It did not shake my faith in the Church and my future within it. I suppose I compartmentalised the different aspects of my experience. But in hindsight I can see that it was my first wobble on a path that I had thought was a certain future.

Four

Turning Away

Life settled back down after Bindoon. I continued as an altar boy and attended Mass numerous times a week. It continued to provide me with a sense of purpose: steps along the way of my journey towards inevitable priesthood.

When I turned 13, I started walking the long way home from church. By coincidence, some of the girls walked that way as well. Yep, just a coincidence. Some days the girls talked to me. Most days, us boys just talked among ourselves about the girls we liked.

Around this time, Dad built a new house for the family in the next suburb, giving me an excuse to start riding my bike up and down a nearby street where a girl named Carmel Long lived. If Carmel Long had ever walked out front to speak with me or even called out my name, I would probably have just kept on riding. I was 13 and had no idea what to say or do. I just felt compelled to be close to her.

This compulsion was the first spark of a slow and confusing change of direction for me. Lying in bed one night I had a moment of clarity: *I am attracted to girls.*

Which led to the next moment of clarity: *If I'm attracted to girls, I can't be a priest.*

With this revelation, Dad's deal with God started to look a little shaky.

The change in me was slow but deliberate. I ceased my altar boy duties and stopped going to Mass on weekdays. It wasn't dramatic and my family seemed to accept it as part of my growing up, but I knew what it meant: my assumed destiny was not to be. I was going to have to find a new future. It wasn't a crisis: I still loved God; I just liked Carmel Long more.

After a couple of years on this new road of slow withdrawal, events outside my control would force me onto a faster track away from God. It was the mid-1950s: the McCarthy era, and a divisive time in the liberty and mindset of Australians. 'Reds' were 'under the bed' and to call somebody a communist could all but destroy their career.

My father was a working-class man who'd realised his dream and been elected as a Labor Senator for Western Australia in 1950. He was also loyal to the Catholic Church. Unsurprisingly, the Church was anti-communist, but it perceived the Labor Party to be tolerant of communism. My father was caught in the middle.

When the Labor Party – the party of unions and workers – split over the fear of communist infiltration, many Catholics left Labor to start the staunchly anti-communist Democratic Labor Party (DLP). It was the best thing that ever happened to the governing Liberal Party. Suddenly, the opposition party had almost no Catholics left in federal parliament because they'd all defected to the DLP. It gifted power to the conservatives for the better part of two decades.

A Boy and his God

My dad tried to stay true to the Labor Party and to the Church, but something had to give. The Church turned on him. One day at Mass, his character and his politics were attacked from the pulpit by different priests who branded him a communist. Mum and Dad walked out of the Church both literally and figuratively. They vowed never to return and would remain in exile from it until their final days. And with their withdrawal from weekly Mass came mine.

But that wasn't to be the end of this bitter plague on my family. It then spread to my school. My headmaster and his sidekick tried to humiliate me constantly. On one occasion, a visiting priest came into the class and the sidekick, Brother Doyle, said, 'Father, we've got a communist in our class. Willesee, stand up and explain to Father Connolly why you are a communist.'

I wasn't mature enough to just tell him I wasn't a communist and sit down. I tried to explain my father's position and got in a big muddle. It was an awful period. I became the butt of class jokes. It was a stream of humiliation. I was frequently sent out of the classroom. They didn't need a reason, just: 'Get out, Willesee! Get out!'

One such day, while I was out in the corridor, the headmaster, Brother Murphy, came by.

'You're out of the class again, Willesee. You're such a troublemaker.'

Bang! He floored me with a right hook. I was tempted to get up off the ground and fight back. I was 15 and just getting big enough to contemplate such a course, but I could see some little kids peering out the window at us. I don't think I even told my parents.

Having no grounds to expel me, they eventually forced me out of the school with deceitful marking of my exam papers.

I went from being consistently in the top three students in my year to consistently scoring 49 per cent in just about every test I sat.

Two older Christian brothers, Brother Hyland and Brother Keane, were good teachers and good men. They tried to keep me in the system, offering places in other schools, even a scholarship at the Christian Brothers' only private school in Perth, Aquinas.

But I'd had enough.

I turned my back on the Christian Brothers and the Church and said goodbye to God for what I then believed would be forever.

Part Two

The Making of a Sceptic

Five

A New Religion

Faced with the prospect of repeating Year 11 after my incredible run of 49 per centers, I left school behind. I was blind when it came to my future. I had no idea what I wanted to do as a career. I just wanted to play footy, drink beer and chase girls. Though I was much better at the first two than the last. I had very low self-esteem and couldn't even bring myself to ask a girl to dance.

Dad helped me get a job at the GPO as a trainee accountant. I spent a year there. It was boring beyond belief. Hour after hour was spent signing forms, stamping things and shuffling paper. After that, I knew I was in trouble and that I'd better get a move on or I'd end up going nowhere fast. I started looking further afield. The one thing that the public service job taught me was that I needed some excitement in my life. I knew that whatever job I did, it was going to have to be exciting.

I started combing the job classifieds. There was one ad for a cadet patrol officer in New Guinea and another for a cadet newspaper reporter for West Australian newspapers. I applied for both jobs and, somehow, got offered both.

I chose journalism and my life came alive. I thought I'd be a good reporter because I was a good writer. As it turned out, I wasn't that good a writer, but I did already possess some of the qualities that would hold me in good stead for 50 years as a journalist. I was genuinely curious – I always wanted to know the truth. I was dogged – I hated going back to the office without the answers. And I was ambitious – I always wanted to achieve something. For me, it wasn't enough to get the story – I wanted to make a difference to the situation. And I was brutally honest in the way I reported the facts and told stories – I hated bullshit and deceit.

After the terrible morass that was working in the public service, the news floor of a daily newspaper was intoxicating. People were yelling, stories were breaking, everything was happening before my eyes and the truth was within my grasp. I couldn't wait to get to work every day. Some days, the chief of staff had no story, so I'd have to go and dig one up myself. I always succeeded. I just seemed to have a nose for it. I could see stories everywhere, and I worked hard to get them. Harder than the next bloke. On my days off, I'd tag along with the police roundsman or go to court. I was like that altar boy a decade earlier – set on my vocation.

By the mid-60s I was in Canberra as bureau chief for the *Daily News*'s bureau of one. I'd married quickly and had a beautiful daughter, Katie, but was already getting restless with my lot at work. As I grew as a reporter, nothing became more important for me than to go to Vietnam. I was an ambitious news breaker, and the conflict in Vietnam, in which Australian troops had been deployed since 1962, was where it was at. Vietnam was the biggest, most important story in the world, and I made it

The Making of a Sceptic

known I'd do anything to cover it. My first chance came when the prime minister of South Vietnam, Nguyễn Cao Kỳ, visited Australia and boasted that some of the mountain areas had been cleared of Viet Cong. When challenged on that, he said he'd take a reporter back on his own plane to prove it. I wasn't the reporter he had in mind, but I was determined to get on that plane.

When, on Friday 27 January 1967, the *Canberra Times* ran a headline: 'REPORTERS ON WAY TO WAR', I was one of them – a correspondent for the *Daily News* and for the 14 radio stations that made up the Macquarie Network.

As we flew into Vietnamese airspace, an old Douglas DC-3 lumbered underneath our plane and American jets whizzed past leaving us shuddering in their wake. I looked out the window and got my first glimpse of Vietnam. It was dry season, but there were a multitude of round dams reflecting bright discs of light up at us. Only later did it occur to me that the 'dams' were in fact craters left from B-52 bombing runs.

At first, our every interaction in Vietnam was a set-up and we reporters saw only what the United States military wanted us to see. We'd sit through presentations and press briefings and emerge blinking into the seamy Saigon afternoon wondering, *What the hell was all that about?*

To get free United States military taxis around Vietnam, you had to play ball. I'd apply for a car for a future date and the Americans would respond, 'That's great, we've got a big show [another interminable bullshit press briefing] in the Mekong Delta that day.' Even if we didn't want to sit through a day of pompous speeches, we'd have to in order to get where we wanted to go for a real story.

On one of our daily excursions, our hosts flew us over a desert of flattened and defoliated land that left nowhere to hide.

It was their way of demonstrating to us that the area had been subdued. They explained that before napalming the area they had put up posters warning the residents of what was about to come, inviting them to leave and move to new accommodation that had been set up for them.

Our plane landed and we were taken to tour this 'accommodation' – huge chicken-wire jails full of women, children and old men. Our hosts declared that there was no Viet Cong within a hundred square miles. I couldn't help but notice that all the women seemed happy. Sure, they were perhaps getting more food than they were accustomed to and they weren't going to be hurt, but if the allied forces had wiped out the area and killed all the men of fighting age, surely there would have been grief. There was none. I could only conclude that their men were still out there, carrying on the fight. It was the first time that I thought through the propaganda and saw it for the nonsense it was.

My first brief trip to Vietnam ignited something inside me. I left the *Daily News* and went to television, first as the Canberra correspondent for the ABC's bold experiment in current affairs, *This Day Tonight,* then as host of its revamped golden child, *Four Corners*. And it was in this role that I was able to get back to Vietnam for three more stints.

And while the public's mood about the war had changed, the American propaganda hadn't. At one of their 'big shows' in a small village hall, I couldn't bear it any longer. I'd sat through hours and hours of speeches, mostly in Vietnamese, and needed to get out to clear my head. I went for a walk along a path through a disused rice paddy when a man in black pyjamas jumped out about forty metres in front of me, pointed his AK-47 rifle at me and motioned me into the jungle.

I froze.

The Making of a Sceptic

I'd had good mates killed by the Viet Cong and others imprisoned in Viet Cong tunnels, held in the ground for months on end until they were just husks of the men they'd once been. I knew the consequences of falling into enemy hands.

For 20 seconds, this Viet Cong and I simply stared each other down. Eventually, my brain thawed from its initial terror and sputtered into action. It occurred to me that when this man first loomed into view pointing his gun at me, he was in charge and I was looking death in the eye. He had me. But as the seconds ticked by, so his authority receded. Now, 20 seconds into our stand-off, the expression on his face was different. He was losing confidence.

I told myself, *Calm down and think. If he's going to shoot you, he's going to shoot you and he hasn't shot you yet. Why not? Why is he losing confidence? He must have friends in the jungle. And he knows there's a stack of American and South Vietnamese diplomats and soldiers just over the ridge who are going to come running if they hear a shot. The Americans will probably call in air support and he and his mates will get killed.*

I'll never know if I was right or not, but his eyes told me it was something like that. He'd started out snarling, *Get in there!* Now it was, *Please get in there?*

So I turned around and walked away. It was the bravest thing I ever did in my life.

Step after step I resisted the urge to turn around. I imagined his friends arguing with him, *Why didn't you shoot him?* But I knew he couldn't. This was my one and only chance of survival. I had to take it.

I walked back into the tent where the speeches were still droning on. The crew were there but I didn't say anything about what had just happened to me. I didn't want to explain it. I'd just gone within a whisker of losing my life, but I said nothing.

On the same trip, a similar thing happened another time I left a boring presentation and went for a walk . . . in a live minefield. I was saved by some Marines who called out to me from a foxhole and had me turn around and walk back – very slowly – retracing my barely discernible footprints. I'd gone out for a walk because I was fretting that I didn't have a story. I never went back to the office without a story. The whole point of the ceremony I'd walked out of was that they'd cleaned the Viet Cong out of the area.

I said to one of the Marines who'd just saved me, 'We've been sent here because you guys have cleaned this area of Viet Cong.'

'Is that right?' one of them responded. 'We killed seven Charlies in this field last night.'

Again, I told no-one about this. When we returned to our hotel that night, I went out on the verandah with a drink and a cigarette and I sat there in silence trying to make sense of it all. I failed. I couldn't claim to know what life was all about. I just knew I needed to find a story.

Six

A Sceptic is Born

Having had great success working for ABC's current affairs programs throughout the late '60s, in 1971, I moved into commercial television. Soon I was producing and presenting nightly national current affairs programs and hosting some of Australian television's most successful shows.

First it was as founder, producer and anchor of *A Current Affair* for the Nine network. In 1974, I moved to Channel 10 to host a Sunday night interview program, *The Mike Willesee Show*. The following year, I was at Channel 7 doing a weekly interview program called *Willesee* and hosting the first season of *This Is Your Life,* before I dived back into the nightly current affairs whirlwind with *Willesee at 7.*

Life was great. Everything just seemed to go right for me. At work, it didn't seem to matter the network or format. Ratings ramped up and money rolled in. I was divorced and had remarried a beautiful woman, Carol. We had a beautiful new baby, Amy, and more on the way. It seemed like I was blessed. Not that I would have put it that way.

Barely a week went by where *Willesee at 7* didn't expose some crank, hoaxer or charlatan, or unveil the scam behind some elaborate visual or financial deception duping ordinary people out of their money. My reputation was as a journalist who sought truth, uncovered deceit and asked hard questions to find hard answers. All while trying to be entertaining.

In the mid-70s, there was a lot of press coming out about a miracle waterfall with magical powers in New Zealand. People were flying in from all over the world to bathe in it and drink its waters to cure their illnesses.

One of the reporters from *Willesee at 7* was extremely interested in it, so we agreed to cover the story. I had reason to believe that this reporter believed too easily and didn't question enough, so before I gave his trip the go ahead, I sat him down and gave him some serious advice.

'Shut up and pay attention,' I said. 'Stuff this up and you'll lose your job. You've got to get it right. You've got to get accurate information.'

He insisted he could be objective about it, so I authorised the trip, and he left for New Zealand the next day. I heard a few mixed reports while he was away, but I knew what advice I had given him, and I was confident he would heed my threats. But on his return, it was clear that he had been taken in by the miracle fountain. He did have footage, yes, but it was of a child who allegedly couldn't walk being carried into the water on one side of the fountain, then standing and walking across the sand into his father's outstretched arms on the other side. 'It was amazing,' the reporter said to me, 'the most incredible thing I've ever seen in my life.'

The Making of a Sceptic

'Oh yeah?' I said. 'What did you do when you saw this kid walk out of the water?'

'Well, I was filming,' answered the reporter.

'I'll tell you what you were doing,' I bit back. 'You were jumping into the waterfall, weren't you?'

There was a short, uncomfortable silence.

'How did you know?' he said, going white.

'I know you, mate. You're an idiot. Just like anyone who believes this crap.'

This was the macho world of '70s television, so I really let him have it. I interrogated him: What was the name of the man who helped the kid into the water? He didn't know. What proof did he have that the child could not previously walk? He merely said that everyone had said so. I was incensed that a reporter of mine could have been so naïve, and waste so much time.

Finally, after really tearing him apart, I made a decision.

'You are going to go back to New Zealand to report from the location again,' I told him. 'But this time, I will be delivering the information to you and you will report it accurately and to the letter. This will be your last job for me, so don't stuff it up!'

I did the research myself and, like many of the exposés of that era, it was straightforward. I spoke to some journo mates across the ditch. They laughed at my questions.

'It's an uncle and his nephew and the uncle's making a fortune out of it,' they told me. 'The kid's not the full quid, but he can walk.'

We exposed the uncle and skewered the miracle waterfall and its miraculous healing waters. Of course, the episode rated gangbusters, another notch in our golden run at the time. And more proof that I was not to be messed with.

★

In 1980, I did a story about water diviners – that is, about those who claim they could locate water without the use of scientific instruments. It started when a Canadian American stage magician and 'scientific sceptic' named James Randi offered a $10,000 reward for anyone who could prove that they could divine water. Randi knew a thing or two about magic and illusions. Performing as 'The Amazing Randi', he'd escaped from a straitjacket strung over Niagara Falls, he'd operated a fake guillotine on stage with the singer Alice Cooper, and he had bent forks with his 'mind'.

Australian entrepreneur Dick Smith chipped in with some cash as did media types Phillip Adams and Richard Carleton along with an unnamed businessman. Between them they topped up the prize to $40,000 for anyone who could successfully complete the challenge they devised. That was a lot of money in 1980.

Smith organised for a sloping paddock to be dug up and for 10 thick white plastic plumbing pipes to be laid out across it, each connected back to a single water source and each able to be turned off and on. They got in 10 of Australia's most respected diviners and showed them where the pipes were laid. The numbered pipes were then covered over. Only one pipe at a time would be turned on, and over the course of the day, the diviners would each get five different opportunities to identify which one was on at that time.

After they'd seen the rules and how everything was to work, the diviners were asked to estimate what success rate they expected to achieve. Most of them thought they'd get it 100 per cent right.

By the end of the day, they'd achieved 22 per cent. If you'd chosen at random you would have expected a 10 per cent success, but 22 per cent was a long way short of their claims for being close to perfect. Similar tests were also done for brass and gold objects for which they had again anticipated success rates up around 100 per cent, but which they did much worse at than the water.

It was hugely fascinating. These were people who made their livings telling people where to sink bores. Hardened bushies believed them and paid accordingly. And they obviously believed in their own powers too. That was clear from the sincerity with which they subjected themselves to this scrutiny. Anyway, no-one got the cash, but the business of querying such claims got a big boost out of it, because the Australian Skeptics was founded as a direct result. Upon formation, they were offering a $100,000 prize to anyone who could prove any sort of paranormal ability. The Australian Skeptics would go on to be great supporters of some of my work, then later, among my greatest detractors. But that was still well into the future. In the meantime, I had a lot of scams to get on with.

Like psychic surgery.

The Filipinos had been practising so-called psychic surgery since the early 1900s via faith healers who would press their fingers into the flesh of someone stricken with tumours, and poke around inside the conscious patient. Their 'healing hands' would seem to enter the body – blood would appear, and the faith healer's hands and fingers would then emerge with some bloody lump of awful-looking flesh, leaving the patient with no scar and totally cured.

Yeah, right.

The American comedian Andy Kaufman, later played by Jim Carrey in the Milos Forman film *Man on the Moon*, attracted a lot of United States tabloid headlines in 1984 when he visited the Philippines for a six-week course of psychic surgery. Kaufman had been diagnosed with a rare form of lung cancer earlier that year. Despite his faith healer claiming to have removed his malignant tumours, Kaufman was dead by May.

The stories about this sham practice had reached Australia in the '80s and were generating headlines. Interestingly, it was tennis champions John Newcombe and Tony Roche, both well-travelled grand-slam winners, who implored me to cover the story to prove it to be true! I was good mates with them both at the time – their legendary playing days were over, and they were enjoying retirement and business interests.

'It's amazing, Mike,' they told me one day after a friendly tennis match. 'We saw it with our own eyes. You've got to tell people about it.'

Knowing me as a sceptic meant they were sure I was the man for the job: if I believed it, who wouldn't?

To me, however, it looked like pure carny fraud, the worst sort of shaman fakery performed by voodoo magicians and third-world confidence tricksters. I was happy to accept the challenge to prove them wrong.

Arrangements were made and we flew to the Philippines and met with the faith healers. We quickly twigged to the hole in the scam being that they never let you see or keep the infected organs they removed.

It turned out they were using fake thumbs full of animal blood to create the blood, and for the illusion of fingers entering flesh, they'd simply fold their digits flat into their palms at the knuckle. The faith healers would then slip chicken giblets into the mess from up their sleeves to make it seem as though diseased flesh was being removed from the human patient.

The Making of a Sceptic

It was nuts, but with the exotic location and the exploitation of people at their most vulnerable, our exposé rated the house down.

It wasn't all about psychics. Sometimes it was about physics. Metaphysics, even. In 1986, the famed race car driver Peter Brock came under our scrutiny when he started making claims about something called a 'Peter Brock Energy Polarizer', which was a $480 gadget for your car that was going to 'rewrite the laws of physics' in improving engine performance. It utilised something called 'orgone energy' for 'aligning the molecules'.

It was only natural that we put it to the test. His system, which he was selling at a healthy margin, consisted of a crystal and two opposed magnets somehow clipped onto the motor. Testing such claims was a bit tricky because Brock said it could only be installed by him or an authorised agent. And that it took time for the benefits to start to come through. How convenient.

We got hold of a car to which Brock had personally fitted a Polarizer, which the owner had then driven for 40,000 kilometres. We put it through a bunch of sophisticated engine-testing apparatus and we also got a couple of experienced motoring writers to test-drive it. Then we took the Polarizer off and tested it again. Neither the owner, the motoring writers, nor the testing apparatus could discern any difference. The 'orgone energy' was all gone.

Of course, Brock's partner Bev Brock accused our physicist of being closed-minded. There were other physicists out there, she said, who agreed with the Brocks that: 'there are energies out there we're just starting to find out about. There's a whole brand of metaphysics out there that they're just starting to understand and give credibility to.'

Well, more than 30 years later we're still waiting for the physicists to catch up to the race-car driver.

In 1986, we uncovered another con which is probably one of the stories I continue to be most remembered for. Uri Geller was a handsome, charismatic Israeli–British citizen who had become world famous for his claimed powers of telekinesis (the ability to alter the physical world with mind power) and telepathy (the transfer of information from one person to another without the use of normal communications). His most famous feat was the bending of spoons without applying any apparent force to them.

By the time we got our hands on Geller, he was already a multi-millionaire from his stage performances and books. We engaged a magician, Ben Harris, to come on the show and pretend to be an acclaimed psychic called Chris Norris. We had him perform some of Geller's greatest hits, like spoon bending and predicting the content of envelopes. Afterwards, he asked viewers to concentrate on their cutlery and broken watches, anticipating that we'd get plenty of calls about viewers' own paranormal phenomena in the suburbs. We did.

After the Chris Norris segment, I interviewed Geller and then handed him over to Norris, who revealed himself as Ben Harris, a magician and sceptic. He accused Geller of using assistants to help him do tricks like stopping Big Ben, the famous London clock, and having them peek inside envelopes for his psychic stage shows. That while he appeared to be just gently rubbing the spoon, he was actually forcing it with his thumb.

'I use the same techniques that you use,' Harris said. 'I learnt from watching you.'

The Making of a Sceptic

'So, what are you telling me?' Geller said, calm and smiling.

'I am telling you that I use your techniques. They are magic tricks and not psychic. And that you are a wonderful, wonderful performer, you are a brilliant magician, however, you are not psychic.'

'If you don't believe I'm psychic and want to believe that I am a magician, that's okay with me too,' responded Geller.

'Uri, how are you going with that drawing?' I interjected.

We had a picture of something in an envelope, I can't remember what, and had asked him to use his psychic powers to replicate it.

'Ah, to be very honest with you,' he said, 'and I am honest at this point . . . I'm not getting it very clearly.'

Geller had drawn a boat, two circles and a triangle.

Harris hit back, claiming that this was a classic Geller technique: draw lots of things and it's bound to look like something to at least claim a partial success.

'Oh no, c'mon Ben!' Geller responded. 'You know, Ben, you sound like a real nice man . . . There are no techniques, Ben! Come on, at the end of the day, if I was using tricks and did have chemicals, or sleight of hand, or bugs in my teeth or peeking into envelopes, I would have been caught a thousand times before.'

'You have been caught many times, Uri.'

And he had too, but it only seemed to make him more popular, more wealthy.

The following year, we learned that an Australian mining company, Zanex Ltd, was paying Geller $350,000 to look for diamonds and gold from an aeroplane above the Solomon Islands. We had a shot of the prime minister of the Solomons holding a bent spoon while cutting the ribbon to open a (conventionally discovered) mine with Geller.

So once again, we got a magician to demonstrate how easy it was to bend a spoon by gently rubbing it. It was all showmanship.

That year, I was awarded the Responsibility in Journalism Award by the Committee for the Scientific Investigation of Claims of the Paranormal (CSICOP) for that story.

And Zanex shares went up.

All this is to say that for every outrageous claim that was being made, there was a test to prove or disprove it. And you could usually have fun with it at the same time. Research was key. It was an approach that had taken me to the top of television land and made me a fortune along the way. I owned a radio station, a racehorse stud, a place on Hamilton Island and a helicopter to scoot between them all. My success was constant reassurance that I was doing the right thing – my life was on the right track. I had a purpose. It was a calling.

Unfortunately, this purpose didn't always translate into a happy domestic life: the hours I worked and my single-minded focus had an impact on my marriage. I wasn't always easy to live with, and I needed a lot of alone time to mentally process the issues I was reporting on. Still, I persisted, certain in the knowledge that the driving force in my life was noble, while presuming all the while that everything on the home front would sort itself and be okay.

My life was full. I certainly had no time for anything that couldn't be proven. That, of course, included religion and God. There was no doubt in my mind that religion was just another scam. There was no God. It was so self-evident it wasn't even worth testing.

Seven

A Chance Meeting

In the late '70s I bought an old farmhouse on 18 acres about two hours north of Sydney as a weekender. My second wife, Carol, and I had three young children, Amy, Jo and Lucy, and my older two, Katie and Michael, would spend weekends with us. We could all walk to a beautiful surf beach nearby. All my success had come from a lot of hard work and that little old farm and its surf beach was my perfect retreat. It was very private; we were not in sight of any neighbour. In fact, we really had only one neighbour, the Tesoriero family who lived across a charming little creek which never ran dry.

In my first encounter with Ron Tesoriero, sparks literally flew. I was sitting by my Australian shrine – a homemade barbecue – relaxing and listening to the bellbirds when I smelled smoke: the distinctive and attractive odour of burning eucalyptus leaves. Straightaway I was transported back to Safety Bay and an emotional collision of pleasure and guilt.

I walked up the hill to witness a man lighting fires in the bushland which backed onto my property. This sort of back-burning was often necessary in winter or spring to reduce the danger of summer bushfires, but what he was doing was potentially dangerous if not done carefully. On this particularly splendid spring day, the conditions were good – I just hoped this bloke knew what he was doing.

Suddenly he climbed my fence and started running. I wasted no time breaking into a sprint and following. The fire had changed direction and was now tearing through a section of bushland on my property. Ron was stomping his boots on burning leaves and grass when I got to him, putting out the embers that had run out of control.

'Sorry,' he said, 'I'm so sorry. I'm your neighbour, Ron Tesoriero.'

'It's okay, mate,' I replied, 'my bush needs cleaning out too.'

We watched the fire like two wise old farmers when, in fact, we were two city boys in our early thirties. And as we watched, the flames stopped advancing.

'I think there's a breeze coming up from behind us,' said Ron. After a while it was clear he was right.

We soon had a great burn-off going, the fire eating up the accumulation of years of dead leaves, the 'fuel' of bushfires. The smoke, however, alerted the local townspeople and brought in a bunch of volunteer firefighters – the heroes of Australia's rural and semi-rural communities. After cautioning us, they agreed the conditions were right to do some controlled burning, so they lit a couple more fires.

More volunteers arrived and by the time night fell, there were controlled fires on three sides of my property. The local pub sent down a couple of cartons of cold beer and the night was as good as the day. I was now a member of the community. About 15 blokes sat around the barbecue talking as millions of sparks covered our bit of the sky. At one point, we caught a snake that tried to join us, and we also talked about organising a new truck for the volunteers. And that's how I met Ron, a lawyer who had developed a successful practice in the area as an expert in local government, zonings and land use. With this expertise he had made some sound land and development investments.

Although I wasn't at the farmhouse full-time, we made it up there as often as we could with the kids. Our three youngest daughters were the same age as Ron's girls so that brought the two families together a lot. Ron and I became good friends. Our conversations, after family, tended to centre around real estate and the business of land. One weekend in the early '90s, however, Ron surprised me by bringing up a topic we'd never discussed before. He trudged up from the creek, grabbed a drink and sat down.

'You used to be a Catholic?' – he said it like it was a challenge.

'Yes, Ron, a long time ago,' I said.

'Do you remember anything about the incident at Fatima?' he asked.

I remembered the tale from my days as an altar boy many moons before.

'A little,' I replied. 'It used to be a pretty big story at school. Three young children in Portugal said the Virgin Mary was talking to them and told them a secret, right?'

'Is that all you remember?'

'That's about it,' I said, 'but I remember the date. 1917. I remember because that was the year my mother was born. What was the secret?'

'I don't know,' he said. 'But the children told people that the Virgin would appear to them again on a certain date. When she did, she spoke of things that had to do with communism, the coming of another, even worse war than that currently raging. She spoke of the future of humanity and what could be done to avert such a dire forecast.'

I wasn't sure where Ron was heading with this but let him go on. He'd clearly been giving it some thought.

'The children were poor and illiterate, but they had the commonsense to express concern to the Virgin Mary that they wouldn't be believed if they spoke of such things to their elders in the village. So, the Virgin promised them that she would perform a public miracle to validate the truth of her appearance and set a date and a time: noon on 13 October 1917.

'The word spread and about 100,000 people turned up. It was bitterly cold and steady rain had fallen all day. Everything and everyone was drenched and muddy. Midday came and went, and nothing happened. Then at solar noon – that is, noon according to the whole planet and not noon according to the local Portuguese – the great mass of grey clouds parted to reveal the sun directly behind it.

'That's when Lucia, one of the three children, shouted: "She's coming!"'

'What happened next was corroborated by many thousands of witnesses and confirmed in myriad newspaper reports the next day,' he went on. 'The sun appeared to spin and hurtle towards the earth. Some said it danced, throwing out beautiful multicoloured lights like a spinning colour wheel. Faces, bodies, trees, umbrellas, rocks and grass all reflected brilliant and changing colours. The sun then spun on its axis. Its rim became scarlet and it shot bursts of flame across the sky.

'Many had by now fallen to their knees in prayer. Surely this celestial display was the end of the world. Suddenly the sun stopped zigzagging across the horizon and for a few seconds a strange wind blew through, drying everyone's sodden clothes

The Making of a Sceptic

and evaporating the mud and the puddles. Witnesses declared that suddenly they felt dry and comfortable and clean.'

I had been listening intently, but I cut in.

'Okay, Ron, what's your point?'

'Well, every person there agreed that was what happened,' he said. 'Over 100,000 people present and everyone within a 30-kilometre radius saw something they'd never experienced before.'

'Ron, I still don't get your point.'

'Okay, Mike. Let me put it this way: if a man is charged with murder and four, or even three, non-related witnesses all say they saw him do it and there are no dissenting witnesses, what happens?'

'I guess he's found guilty.'

'That's right,' said Ron, warming to his argument. 'And here we have three peasant kids making a prediction, 100,000 people turning up and saying they all saw the sun charging out of the sky. Many said they thought they were going to die.'

We sat quietly for a moment. I wasn't sure what Ron wanted me to say – that I thought Fatima was real? That I believed this 80-year-old make-believe story?

'The point is,' he said, 'that by all or any standards of evidence – that phenomena happened. And it's been forgotten. It had to mean something.'

Ron went on, 'The reason I am telling you all this is that one of the three children who the Virgin Mary appeared to, who is central to this story, is still alive. Her name is Sister Lucia and she is an aged nun living in Portugal. With your power and influence, you can interview anyone in the world! Why would you not want to interview her to hear her story first-hand? It's never been done before. It would be a world first.'

Even though the Fatima story made no impact on me and I had no room for such matters in my life, I didn't bother putting a counterargument to Ron that day. I thought he was just riffing.

Eventually, I said, 'Okay, mate, if you line up the interview, then I'll do the story.'

We finished our beers and called it a day.

For the next 10 years, Ron worked on trying to get that interview. He went to Portugal, he went to Rome, but to no avail. He managed to succeed in getting an endorsement from the Catholic Church of Australia for us and a recommendation to Pope John Paul II requesting that we be permitted to interview Sister Lucia. But the Vatican demurred, saying that Sister Lucia has never before been permitted to give an interview and that they did not intend to change that policy. Ron learned that Hillary Clinton had also requested an interview with Sister Lucia, and that she too was declined.

It looked like it wasn't going to happen, but Ron wasn't nearly ready to give up yet. Meanwhile, I didn't give Ron's story another thought. After all, I was Australia's most famous sceptic.

Part Three

Seeds of Doubt

Eight
The Premonition and the Prayer

My last stint as the regular host of *A Current Affair* finished up in 1993. I was bored with the job. I had never loved being stuck in a studio. I longed to be on the road. I had made a lot of money and had nothing left to prove in journalism. I was single again, after my second marriage had failed. The kids were moving on. My eldest two, Katie and Michael, had finished university, Amy had just left school while the younger two, Lucy and Jo, were in high school. I was enjoying the bachelor lifestyle. Life was good.

But in easing back on work, I had time to think. I reflected on the great deal of interest other people seemed to have in my life – especially people I hadn't met before. They'd want to talk about things I'd done in the past – anything from my time in Vietnam to my famous interviews with Quentin Kenihan – the boy with a disability about whom I had made a documentary – or my stoushes with various prime ministers. Or about my money. I couldn't help thinking they were stupid questions. It was all in the past. Gone. Whatever I'd achieved hadn't amounted to much. Everything was so ephemeral. I was bored talking about it.

When I had become a journalist, I was ambitious and hungry: I thrived on the pressure, the chase, whatever it took to run a story down. I had succeeded beyond my own expectations. I was living the dream. But it was starting to feel a little hollow. Like there had to be more.

All that thinking led to the inevitable question: What am I doing now?

Each morning, I'd find myself daydreaming in the shower, saying things like, 'God, I don't know if you're there, but I hope you are because if you are that would make a lot more sense of this world and if you are there, I could do with a hand.' I did not see this as praying. It was more like a mantra. Maybe it was a little cry for help. But it was a start to asking the big question. Why am I here?

I was 51. I figured I had another 20 or 30 years left in me, but I didn't know what I was going to do with it. Play tennis every day? Think of somewhere new to travel every few months? Buy a better bottle of wine? Start a new television show? None of this appealed to me. I had bought into the Sydney Swans AFL team a few years earlier and they took up a lot of my time and passion. But I'd lost interest in doing most of the things that had fuelled my adult life. There was a certain emptiness, emptiness in my future and an emptiness in my past because no matter what I had achieved, that had gone.

For all that, there was one aspect of my old job that I still felt a passion for, and that was being on the road in pursuit of a story. And so that's what I decided to do.

I'd always been fascinated by people living in their traditional ways. My documentary *The Hunting Party*, about a group of Indigenous men living off the land racing across Arnhem Land against a group of special forces soldiers, had been a huge ratings hit back in the early '80s. I thought it would be fascinating to get back on the road and scour the globe for people still living lives untouched by modern civilisation and to document ways of life that would likely soon disappear.

My company, Trans Media, was still a going concern. We'd made a documentary series called *Street Stories* the year before, so it wasn't hard to get a crew together.

The Dinka people of southern Sudan were our first subjects. At the time, southern Sudan was in a seemingly perpetual state of civil war against the north. Some two million Sudanese had already died, half of whom were Dinka.

The aggressors were the Arabs from the north who controlled the government in Khartoum, but not the country. The conflict was older than memory, but this time the weaponry was upgraded – a nasty leftover from the Cold War. Automatic assault rifles, mostly AK-47s, had replaced the swords of the Arabs and the spears of the Africans. The Sudanese government even had an air force and, courtesy of the Russians, some Ilyushin bombers and a handful of MiG jet fighters.

What the Dinka saw, and what sent them into isolation, was that men of all nationalities were coming to their land on camels and in trucks to burn their villages, steal their cattle, rape their women and kidnap their children to sell as slaves. The Dinka had retreated to the farthest fringes of society.

In the Dinka way of life, men and women still walked through their villages unashamedly naked, their children drinking milk straight from the udders of their cows, their adolescent boys drinking blood syphoned direct from the neck veins of their cattle and collected in a horn. There was but one concession to the modern world. AK-47s.

*

It was a beautiful night in Lokichogio, Kenya, in late 1993.

Three of us – cameraman Greg Low, soundie Ralph Steele and I – sat on the high bank of an almost dry river appreciating a cold beer. It would be the last for a few weeks. We discussed flying into this war zone the next day. Ralph was adamant we would be safe. I wasn't as sure – the rebel army had taken over the once-safe international relief agency World Vision camps and their vehicles.

'No problem,' said Ralph when I aired my concerns. 'I met some Kenyan vets.'

Greg and I laughed. 'Vets?'

'Yeah, veterinarians. They help the Dinka with their cattle. The rebels won't bother them, and they'll give us a vehicle.'

It sounded odd, but it made sense. For the Dinka tribe, as with many African tribes, cattle were the centre of their existence. A man was measured by the number of cows he owned; his daughter was measured by the number of cows she could attract as her bride price. And when the Dinka needed favours from their gods, they sacrificed a cow.

Our assignment was a documentary on these great people, the tallest and the darkest in skin colour in the world. They still lived with the same laws, traditions and ceremonies of forgotten ancestors. It was a harsh life with famine and war as constant companions, but it never affected their pride. They called themselves 'man among men'. We were not there to film the war; we were filming despite the war.

The next day, we rendezvoused with the veterinarians as Ralph had planned, and organised to borrow a vehicle from them. We drove into the land of the Dinka following a couple of wheel ruts, looking for a cattle camp, any camp for that matter. The Dinka cattle camps were a seasonal thing where the young men and women would take their cows and goats to the grassy floodplains for the whole of the dry season. The feed was plentiful. Each clan established a different camp.

As we went deeper into the floodplains of the White Nile, the first people we saw were three naked teenage girls. When the girls saw us, they turned and quickly ran back into their *tukul* (thatched hut). We felt embarrassed because we thought they were embarrassed. They had probably never seen white men in their cattle camp, and they may have never seen a vehicle either.

The camp we had stumbled across was almost empty – the youngsters had taken the stock into the bush to forage. The three young women who had taken flight when we appeared now came out of their hut wearing the oldest dresses possible. They led us to a site just outside the camp to pitch our tents. One of the girls attached herself to me and assisted me in any way she could, though she never entered my tent.

Watching the cattle return, each with its own tether and ground peg, was an experience but it was getting dark and we began to hear the first of the lions roaring. We had travelled a long way in the heat of Sudan and were very tired. A campfire was built, and we cooked a quick meal and headed to our tents for an early night.

'No!' shouted our translator. 'You must wait for the dance.'

Greg and Ralph headed for their tents anyway, but I stayed. The hours passed and I struggled to keep my eyes open, but I wanted to stay awake for the performance – I felt that I owed them the courtesy. Every now and then I would hear a distant drum, then another, and another. It was the sound of boys and girls coming from other cattle camps, sometimes miles away.

Finally, amid what seemed like a chaotic set-up, something cohesive started to take shape.

There were more boys than girls, all clothed, with about 10 girls running among the boys, who were all clamouring for their attention. Each girl selected one boy and the boys who missed out clearly showed their displeasure. The girls stood in a line and the 10 boys formed a line facing them. The drums started a slow beat and the girls started moving slowly with the beat. The boys started stomping their feet.

I had waited so long and was so tired. I was thinking, *Is this all it is?*

But then the drums started beating faster and the girls, who looked to be about 14 or 15 years of age, shed their clothes. Naked, they twisted their arms backwards as if their shoulders were double-jointed and started thrusting their pelvises forward to the ever-increasing beat of the drums. The boys, still clothed, were stamping their feet to the same beat. I was both shocked and mesmerised; I had never seen anything like it.

Another thing that struck me was that in this extraordinarily sexual performance, there was not the slightest sense of lust, not even a hint of flirting. The boys and the girls simply ignored each other. And when the drums, having reached a crescendo, stopped, both participants and spectators simply walked away.

I was exhausted but my senses were heightened. I made my way to the tent, but it took me hours to settle. After just one night, I already knew this experience with the Dinka was going to be like nothing I had ever experienced before – and I knew I'd probably never fully understand the way they saw the world. That night, as I battled to sleep, I saw a shadow circling my tent. I got up to go to the toilet, and I realised it was a hyena. Its jowls glistened in the moonlight. My piss could wait.

The next morning after getting ready for the day, I came out of the tent to find Greg and Ralph sitting in a circle with some World Vision staff having a prayer meeting. Greg invited

Seeds of Doubt

me to join them. I declined. It would have been hypocritical. I didn't identify as an atheist, but I didn't know if there was a God and I certainly didn't see the point of praying. The question of God's existence or not was something for others – it was a riddle I just never thought about anymore. I didn't need God. And I doubted He had any need of me. I was far more interested in understanding the ancient traditions of Dinka culture than I was in unlocking any truths from my own.

The footage we got was so good we decided to grow it into a series to be called *The Last Warriors*. We made numerous trips to Africa over the coming years, to observe different peoples across different seasons. In January 1998, we were back in Nairobi, Kenya, and did not need to be told that we had returned for the monsoon season. The city was waterlogged and seemed just one cloudburst away from being completely flooded.

On the morning we were due to depart for Sudan to rejoin the Dinka, Greg and I got in a cab to head to Nairobi's Wilson airport just after dawn. It was an old London cab, a relic of this African country's colonial past, but its charm was lost on us that morning. We were anxious and moving too slowly for my peace of mind.

The trickle of locals walking to work through the muddy roadsides was increasing; their heads down against the drizzle. We passed the Nairobi police station and noticed about 100 people standing outside in the rain. Greg and I exchanged glances: that many people meant there had been trouble overnight. At another time we would have stopped to ask questions, but not today.

We had our own problems to handle. Our sound recordist, Ralph, had volunteered to go ahead of us into Sudan to help plan our next filming schedule with the Dinka. He was staying in one of two permanent camps established in the area by World Vision. The day before, however, rebel soldiers had entered the camp and held the workers at gunpoint. The United Nations had declared a high-level state of emergency, flown in an aircraft with some UN troops, and ordered the evacuation of all expatriate workers to a UN aid base in the north of Kenya.

I'd spoken with a UN official at Lokichogio that night and he was emphatic: 'The evacuation is complete. We got everybody out of there. Your man would have been among them.' When pressed, however, he admitted he did not have Ralph's name on any list and could not tell us where he was. Also, he could not confirm or deny that one or more hostages were being held by the rebels.

To complicate matters, Ralph was carrying a satellite telephone. He had called us in Nairobi during the drama and told us not to worry.

'The problem is between World Vision and the SPLA [Sudan Peoples' Liberation Army],' he said. 'The UN will evacuate the aid workers, but I will be staying.'

I asked him if hostages were being held.

'I don't think so,' he said. 'They are asking questions and they are searching the *tukuls*.' He then added, casually: 'I'm okay as long as they don't find my satellite telephone.'

That was an understatement. To be caught in a war zone with any communication device was to risk being labelled a spy; it was very dangerous.

'Ralph, I'm not very comfortable with you staying there,' I said.

'Don't worry, mate,' he replied, 'I'll see you tomorrow.'

But I was worried. We had been unable to raise him again

on the satellite telephone. 'Tomorrow' was now today and we did not know where he was, and we did not know if he was safe.

We decided to ignore the UN restrictions and fly into Sudan to find Ralph, and hopefully complete filming. But with the Nairobi monsoon, we didn't know if the control tower would allow us to fly out. Nor did we know if we could safely land on the bush airstrip near the camp once in Sudan.

As the cab approached the airport, I scanned the clouds in the hope of seeing an aircraft in the air. Greg read my mind: 'It's probably too early for any take-offs.'

I nodded. I tried to think of something funny to say to lighten the mood, but nothing came to mind.

Wilson Airport is an unimposing place – it is just two runways and a collection of single-storey buildings. We pulled in at the terminal, which housed immigration and customs, to the west of which were two big wire gates where a long line of trucks and pick-ups waited, all heavily loaded with some type of green leafy vegetable.

The sight of this rickety convoy brought back bad memories: I had first seen it when I had flown from Wilson Airport to Somalia five years earlier. The green leafy vegetable was in fact a drug called *khat*, pronounced 'chat'. Starvation was a major weapon in the war being waged in neighbouring Somali. There were periods when it was impossible to fly food in, and even when aid agencies could get food in, much of it was stolen by warlords. People were dying of starvation in tens of thousands.

Khat, however, was flown in daily. The Somali gunmen relied on it. Food occasionally got in, *khat* always. *Khat* is a drug that needs to be chewed fresh and I saw it on sale in the markets of Mogadishu and Baidoa every day, on the same days as I saw people, mostly children, dying from starvation.

It was a euphoric drug and there was always more shooting after the *khat* hit the markets around midday.

When the gates opened on this soggy morning, the drug convoy bypassed immigration and customs and each vehicle drove directly to its designated light aircraft on the tarmac. There was no paperwork; the only paper which changed hands was currency. In the context of the Somali war, it was an evil trade.

We had no visas or papers allowing us to enter Sudan, but the officials let us through and we walked down to the small terminal of our charter company, where we were cheered to see the first aircraft of the day taxi for take-off; it meant the weather was now unlikely to stop us. The terminal was yet to open so we settled down to wait. Two Kenyan missionaries approached us asking our destination and their luck was in. We were heading their way and we offered them a ride.

Several more aircraft took off in the pouring rain and our confidence started to increase: we would fly, we would find Ralph and we would get on with our assignment. But when the terminal opened, we hit an unexpected obstacle.

'Your flight has been cancelled,' the general manager informed us.

'Who cancelled it?' I asked.

'Well, we did,' he said. 'The United Nations has declared a high-level state of emergency in the area you want to fly to, so we had to cancel it.'

'The UN officials don't have the authority to stop us,' I argued. 'This flight is illegal anyway. We have no permission to enter Sudan which is why we're trying to fly in under the radar.'

His eyes widened. 'Look, I've only been in this job a week. I'll have to check with my boss.'

Greg and I knew his boss, a 40-something-year-old woman who had helped fund her small fleet by flying *khat* into Somalia during the war. We had both flown with her numerous times.

'Your company has already flown us into Sudan under these conditions on three occasions,' I said. 'Your boss was the pilot each time. Now, do you have an aircraft available?'

He hesitated a moment, but then conceded, 'Yes we have an aircraft, but now I'll have to find a pilot.'

Ralph was on our minds and we were getting anxious – it was a bad day to have 'one of those days'. We settled down to wait, a wait that ended up being several hours, but which under the circumstances felt much longer. The pilot arrived about 10 am. We gathered our gear and our missionary passengers and boarded. It was a twin-engine turboprop configured for about 10 passengers up the front, space for cargo and a couple of seats at the back. Greg and I chose the back seats for the extra leg room. All the take-offs that morning had been from the one runway, but our pilot taxied to the start of the second runway. There was no wind, so it didn't seem to matter. We sat waiting for clearance and I recall feeling relieved that we were finally about to go.

But as we sat there, I was suddenly hit with a profound conviction that the plane was going to crash.

I tried to dismiss it as some weird manifestation of my anxiety and tiredness, but it wouldn't budge. It was an experience that I could not relate to, nor understand, but it was as real as a sudden migraine attack. It was a premonition and I did not believe in premonitions. Strangely, it was not accompanied by any sense of fear, just confusion: should I tell Greg? What would I tell Greg? Will he think that I have lost my nerve for going into combat zones? Should I get off the plane? What about my responsibility to Ralph?

Not panic, just confusion. I did not think the plane *might* crash; in my bones I knew it *would* crash.

But I did nothing.

Well, nothing that Greg would have noticed. I said my first prayer in 35 years; a prayer to a God whose existence I was quite uncertain about.

'Father, I place Greg and myself in your hands.'

The pilot pushed the throttles forward and we were pressed back into our seats as the plane gathered pace down the runway. There was a sudden impediment to the acceleration, almost as if he had applied the brakes, but almost immediately we picked up speed again. It happened a second time: we sped up, then slowed down. I looked out the window. Floodwaters were running from right to left across the runway.

Greg and I looked at each other. We both knew the pilot should abort the take-off, but instead, he was persisting: faster, slower, faster, slower. Then he pulled the nose up and we took off. The stall alarm immediately started beeping, but we continued to climb. The more we climbed, however, the more the attitude of the plane – that is, its orientation in the air – deteriorated. We were too far nose up and tail down. There was a glimmer of silence when the plane seemed to be suspended in the air. But then we began to fall: spinning and vibrating, tail first.

I can remember only one thought: *I was right!*

My head banged against the cabin wall. I could not see, I could not think, and I can't remember hitting the ground. I soon became aware that the plane was again horizontal and on the ground. But still moving, spinning, like a child's spinning top; too fast for me to be able to see. As the momentum slowed, it was clear we were hitting obstacles. When the plane finally stopped, one of the turbo engines was screaming and there was a lot of smoke. I experienced my first burst of fear: the aircraft was going to explode.

Greg was closest to the door and without leaving his seat he started wrestling with the door; it was jammed. There was no sign of the pilot. Greg forced the door open and the two missionaries ran out, clearly panicked, and with good reason. There were no stairs, but they did not have to jump: the bottom half of the plane had either been torn off or was buried in the mud.

I looked at Greg to see if he needed help.

He had his camera in his hands and said: 'I'm okay, you go first.'

I went through the door. Outside I saw we were in the bush; the turbo was still screaming, and the threat of an explosion and fire seemed even greater than from inside. A few moments later, I realised with horror that Greg had not followed me out. I ran back to the plane. His seatbelt buckle had jammed, but just as I came back in the door, he forced it open. We bolted out, but this time I ran into a thorn tree and picked up about a dozen thorns in my hands. We quickly moved a safe distance from the aircraft.

After some searching, we saw the pilot standing about 100 metres away in the bush; the plane was about 50 metres past the end of the runway. The propellers were partially stuck in the mud and the blades were badly twisted. The port wing had a large hole in the middle and the starboard wing had started to tear from the fuselage.

The plane had knocked down about 20 small trees, maybe more, and the track it had created from the end of the runway looked like it had been ploughed; it was strewn with the metal wreckage of the bottom half of the plane, including wheels and tyres.

Fire engines arrived and stopped a very safe distance from the crash. The first aimed its foam cannon and fired: a small blob of white foam landed a few metres in front of the truck. Nobody was in danger, so there were a few nervous laughs. A man who said he was a doctor arrived, carrying a bag just big enough for his lunch. He insisted that Greg and I be taken to hospital. I asked him why.

'Because I think you have a ruptured pancreas,' he said.

'Why?' I asked, perplexed at his instant diagnosis.

'Because it's happened in other aircraft crashes.'

The smoke eased and the turbo finally stopped. Greg reclaimed his camera from amid the debris, to take some footage of the wreck, and I retrieved our baggage. The aircraft was never to fly again, and the pilot would lose his licence.

We were driven back to the terminal in a small vehicle. The new manager was agitated. 'That aircraft arrived back from Johannesburg only yesterday after a complete refit,' he said with his head literally in his hands. Then, looking up, he exclaimed, 'Oh, I'm sorry. Are you all right? Is there anything I can do?'

'Yes,' I said, 'you can get us another aircraft and a real pilot. We have to get there today and we've lost a lot of time.'

He agreed and we dictated a statement on the crash. The good news was that our new pilot was to be his boss. We were sitting in the lounge with coffee, waiting for her arrival, when Greg's mobile phone rang. It was our man, Ralph.

'Where are you?' he demanded.

'We're still at Wilson Airport,' said Greg. 'We've been in a plane crash.'

'Well, what time are you getting here?'

'I thought you might like to know that we're okay,' Greg said.

Seeds of Doubt

'Good. What time are you getting here?'

That was Ralph: when there was a job to be done, there were no frills, no niceties. We enjoyed working together as a team. He explained that he had been physically forced onto the UN evacuation flight so we arranged to meet him in Lokichogio, Kenya, where we would now need to spend the night. We had lost a day, but it would give me a chance to find a nurse and have the thorns removed from my hands. They seemed to be toxic and were quite painful.

Our pilot arrived, and our plane was prepped on the first runway – where a take-off would still be possible. Greg and I boarded our replacement flight sombrely and buckled up (the missionaries had declined the offer of a second attempt). While in the air, I finally had time to think about the plane crash. As a journalist, I had been in a few threatening situations, mostly in Vietnam, but I had never been hurt. My first reaction to today's crash had been that this was just one more near-miss. It was luck.

Then I thought of the premonition. I remembered arguments where I had presented a rational case against the existence of such things. 'You hear about the guy who refused to go on his scheduled flight,' I had said. 'The plane crashes, killing all on board. But there would be tens of thousands of people out there who'd refused to get on flights over the years because of what they claim to be a premonition. But their planes don't crash, so you never hear of these so-called premonitions.' End of argument.

But as I sat with Greg on that flight to Lokichogio, there now seemed to be a gaping hole in my argument. What else could I call that feeling I had on the tarmac: I'd never had such a feeling before. It was strong; it was vivid; I had believed it, and the plane had crashed.

And I had said my first prayer in my adult life to a God whose existence I doubted. I sensed that all this should mean something; that there should be a message. But nothing came. I did say a short thankyou to my maybe God. And that was it.

Back in Sydney, I immersed myself in editing *The Last Warriors*. I thought it was one of the best things I'd ever done. My enthusiasm was spreading to everybody involved. I told no-one of the premonition. Or the prayer.

Nine

A Favour for a Friend

When I next carried my bag into the departure lounge of Sydney's international airport, I was holding a ticket not to Africa, but to South America.

Six months after the plane crash, I was now flying to Bolivia to meet a woman named Katya Rivas, and I did not know why. I knew the circumstances and the purpose of the trip, but I did not know why I had agreed to go. The prospects of getting a story were so slim that I hadn't even bothered convening a team for the trip – I was travelling alone. No camera crew and a disturbing absence of the excitement I was accustomed to enjoying on each new assignment.

After take-off I was offered a glass of French champagne, but it seemed flat. Was it just my mood or were there some bubbles missing? I reflected on the chain of events that had led to me making this trip.

It had been a couple of years since I'd sold the property on the Central Coast, and I hadn't seen a lot of my old friend and neighbour, Ron Tesoriero. I did know, however, that he had maintained his interest in incidents where God's intervention was claimed, an interest sparked years earlier by the Fatima tale. He'd since begun to explore other claims – other 'interventions' from God, as he called them. He had started travelling extensively to look into the different claims, and after each trip he would enthusiastically relate what he had seen.

Ron was a friend, and he had been a great neighbour and helped me out with the law a few times, so out of respect for him, and for our friendship, I would listen to what he had to say. Yet despite his enthusiasm and passion, I was not interested in investigating the claims as a journalist. They just didn't grab me. I had put my own experience of a premonition to the back of my mind, and got on with researching subjects firmly in the physical realm.

'I have investigated many claims of the supernatural,' I would tell him, 'and they are all so similar. Money, ego or cult, or all three. And I have never found any to be authentic.'

But Ron persisted.

The link to South America started in 1995, when Ron called me to tell me about a phenomenon he had been looking into there.

'Mike,' he said earnestly, 'I am working on a very interesting story. In Bolivia there is a statue of Christ which has been weeping tears and bleeding.

'I have filmed it happening,' he went on. 'And we have taken samples to laboratories and the substance has passed the test for human blood.'

He then paused, letting the silence hang like a challenge.

'Of course it's human blood,' I replied lightly. 'What other sort of blood would you place on a statue? Or *in* a statue, if you wished to fool people?' Open, shut.

'The blood does not come from inside the statue,' he said,

'we have put the statue through a CAT scan and there is no orifice. It can't come from within.'

'And,' he added, 'we filmed it for several hours so that nobody could place anything on the statue.'

I told Ron that this story sounded more promising than the others and invited him to keep me informed. But in truth I believed I would be able to identify the fraud if I looked into it.

In 1996, he called again.

'This story is growing,' he said. 'There is a woman in Bolivia who says she is receiving messages from Jesus and they appear to be authentic.'

'Ron . . .' I started to say, ready with questions as always.

'Wait,' he said, 'even the city's archbishop says the messages are theologically sound.'

'What city?' I asked.

'Cochabamba,' he replied.

'Isn't that the same place you said the statue of Christ was bleeding?'

'Yes, it is.'

'Doesn't that sound like too much of a coincidence, Ron?'

'Why?' he asked.

'I don't know. It just seems a bit much for a cluster of miracles to be happening in a small city in Bolivia, of all places. What happened to your investigation of the blood?'

'Well, that's a bit of a mystery,' he said. 'The blood was human and fresh and laboratories in the United States and Sydney found it contained human DNA. It is human blood. But the blood does not have a human genetic profile.'

'Ron, I have to say that sounds a bit dodgy to me.'

'On the contrary,' he said. 'For example, if you had placed your blood on the statue, we would have a clear DNA profile.'

I could see his point.

'Okay, so tell me about the woman.'

'Her name is Katya Rivas,' he said. Ron then went on to describe Katya to me: she was an intelligent but relatively uneducated woman. She had no qualifications or training to write at the theological level of the messages she had been scribing. The messages were also beautifully written – the author would not just need to know a great deal about theology but would also need to possess a great way with words.

'Mike, it's a big ask for an uneducated housewife,' Ron concluded.

I had other ideas. Just because Katya was the person claiming to write the messages, it didn't mean she was.

I told Ron that I could see no reason to investigate. It just wasn't catching my interest. The messages could be from anyone: however theologically sound they might be was a fairly subjective matter. I didn't want to get involved in something that would likely turn out to be a waste of time. As far as I was concerned, there was no story here.

Another year rolled by and Ron was on the phone again. It was about mid-1997.

'This story just keeps growing, Mike. The woman I told you about, Katya Rivas, is now receiving the stigmata; the wounds of Christ on the cross.'

I knew a little of the phenomenon of the stigmata. Back in 1224, St Francis of Assisi had been praying at La Verna when five bleeding wounds appeared on both his hands and feet and on his side. An angel supposedly told St Francis: 'I have given you the stigmata which are the emblems of my Passion, so that you may be my standard bearer.'

St Francis bore that standard and bore the pain thereafter, often bleeding from the same five wounds, before dying two years later.

Seeds of Doubt

Another, more recent, example had come via an Italian Capuchin priest, Padre Pio, who experienced the same five wounds for over fifty years. His lesions were repeatedly examined by doctors who swarmed from all over the world to study him in the name of science, and worshipped by thousands who flocked to attend his sermons. During Mass, Padre Pio took great care to conceal his lesions under clothing, but the blood would penetrate any bandages or gloves he donned. When the wounds finally healed just before his death in 1968, no scarring was left, not even the slightest blemish. At Padre Pio's official canonisation in 1999, Pope John Paul II said: 'His stigmata were the work and sign of divine mercy, which redeemed the world by the cross of Christ. Those open bleeding wounds spoke of God's love for everyone.'

Not that any of these stories had swayed me into believing them.

'What evidence do you have?' I asked Ron, 'I mean, *hard* evidence?'

Ron told me that he had obtained film footage of Katya experiencing the stigmata on 4 July 1997 at Tarija in Bolivia. He said that he had carefully perused the recording, from which it was evident that Katya had experienced a series of puncture wounds across her forehead, that her hands and feet began to bleed in locations where we understand that Christ was nailed to the cross. The wounds started from nothing and progressively grew and got worse between noon and 3 pm. By the next morning, wounds that normally would take weeks to heal were almost completely healed. Ron said that he had interviewed on film the person who recorded the event and each of the people who were present. Their testimonies all accorded.

However, I was still not prepared to believe that someone could genuinely have the stigmata.

One more year and one more call, and this time I caved in.

Ron challenged me, 'Why do you give a negative opinion about the cases that I am working on and telling you about? You are not even willing to look at the facts. I thought that the role of a good journalist was to look at the facts and *then* give your opinion. Why don't you at least go and check out the facts and then tell me what you think? If these stories turn out to be true, it is a case of God intervening in human affairs with possible implications for humanity. Is that not sufficient reason to check it out?

'Better still,' he went on, 'prove me wrong.'

So there I was, flying east across the Pacific at around 40,000 feet, wondering – not for the first or last time – why I said yes to this at all.

I thought I had a reasonable chance of finding some truths about the bleeding statue, and about the woman Katya Rivas and her 'stigmata'. That was because in similar-sounding cases, I had found answers. But if and when I did find these strange happenings in Bolivia to be a fraud, what would I do about it? Apart from upsetting my friend, I would almost certainly do nothing. Did anybody really care that another bunch of incredible claims, supernatural claims, were false? I thought not. It was a non-story. And if I failed to prove fraud, I knew that such a failure did not naturally flow to a proof of truth. Another non-starter. Oh well, I *was* on the plane and I would be in Cochabamba in 16 or 17 hours.

Coming in to land, the plane dipped over a wall of hills and I could see that Cochabamba was in a basin encircled by rugged hills. Looking out to the left, I was startled to see a huge stone figure of Christ, surely bigger than the one in Rio de Janeiro.

It stood in a commanding position overlooking the city. I had to concede that if God was 'intervening', then this looked as good a place as any.

As I walked across the tarmac to the humble terminal, I spotted Ron standing with another man beyond the wire fence – Ron was carrying a large video camera on his shoulder and appeared to be filming my arrival. There was no baggage carousel, not that I had expected one, just an overcrowded room with porters bringing the luggage in. Once I had grabbed my bag, I went to meet Ron, who welcomed me and introduced me to his companion, a professor and doctor named Ricardo Castanon. Ricardo, Ron explained, was a psychologist specialising in relating chemical activity in the brain to human behaviour. The Catholic Church had engaged him to look into what was taking place in Bolivia, and since then, Ron and Ricardo had spent some time studying the Bolivian cases together.

Ricardo was warm and genial; the conversation as we made our way to his car was light and amiable. But beneath the surface, I was in work mode. My attitude, hopefully well hidden, was one of suspicion: I believed that fraud was the most likely answer awaiting. It was just a matter of how I was going to show it. The bleeding statue presented as an investigative challenge that I was accustomed to. The stigmata claims, however, were new to me. The only way you could disprove such a thing would be to witness it from beginning to end. As for the 'messages' the Bolivian woman was claiming to be receiving and transcribing from God: well, I had little doubt that I would see what Ron Tesoriero had seen. An uneducated woman writing long and detailed messages that would prove to be theologically sound and of literary quality. But I would be seeking to find out who the true source of her material was.

That was to be my starting point for the whole investigation, such that it was.

As we drove to the hotel, I asked about the enormous statue of Christ I had seen from the air.

'Do you like it?' Ricardo asked.

'It's very imposing,' I said. 'It looks even bigger than the one in Rio.'

'I think it is only one or two centimetres taller,' he laughed. 'If you are going to build one like Rio's, of course you have to make it a little bit bigger – like the Japanese Eiffel Tower.'

Ricardo Castanon was clearly highly educated, but his background was unusual: a psychologist enlisted by the Catholic Church to investigate the mental state of a woman who said Jesus was talking to her. Nevertheless, I quickly took a liking to him: he was intelligent and warm. But by the time we had arrived at the hotel, he was number one on my list of suspects of who might be collaborating in this fraud.

'Doesn't look like a hotel,' I said as we pulled up outside an old church with three or four beggars on the steps: women wearing little bowler hats and multi-layered skirts. Ron pointed out an old two-storey building adjacent to the church with a belltower.

'It used to be a monastery,' said Ricardo. 'I think you would not give it five stars, but it is comfortable.'

Ron and Ricardo suggested I rest for a few hours.

'I will pick you up later,' Ricardo said, 'and we will take you to meet Katya.'

Ten

Is Seeing Believing?

I had met plenty of important, impressive or downright frightening people throughout my years as a journalist. But I rarely felt nervous ahead of time — only for the real VIPs. Even when I met the Queen of England, I was so preoccupied with the traffic on the way there that I forgot all about my nerves. There were no such traffic problems to divert me on my way to meet Katya Rivas that afternoon in Cochabamba. I was surprised to realise that I was feeling apprehensive, even intimidated.

'This is her street,' said Ricardo, as we turned off a main road and onto an unmade dirt street. The houses lining the potholed road were quite modest, but had high walls with barbed wire or broken glass atop them, which suggested the area was unsafe. Ricardo slowed to avoid some cows wandering unattended down the street; we saw no people. As we pulled in, I noted that Katya and her husband Hugo's house was typical of the street, but without the fortification. It had a small front yard which was paved in concrete. I observed a small car, maybe 10 years old, parked by the side of the house. As we made our way to the door, I was surprised by the presence of a strong fragrance, like women's perfume. I recalled that Ron had mentioned a rose-like fragrance which was sometimes noted around Katya and I was immediately suspicious. But Ricardo and Ron showed no sign that they had even smelled it. Nor did they appear to be watching for a reaction from me. I said nothing.

Katya opened the door to us and gave me a friendly greeting along with Ron and Ricardo, before leading us through a small sitting room to the kitchen. Two other people were already seated at the kitchen table and Katya resumed a conversation with them as we joined them, leaving us to wait while they wound up their discussion. They were speaking in Spanish, but it suited me to be out of the conversation and simply observing. The visitors did not seem to be acting in any obsequious way towards Katya – the three of them appeared to be speaking as equals.

Katya was absolutely ordinary-looking. I am not quite sure what I had been expecting, but, at 53, she was a fuller-figured woman with a serious and dignified look. She had a quietly attractive face and wore little make-up. Her eyes were pretty and her smile pleasant. Her hair was short and simple, and she wore slip-on house shoes and plain and modest clothing.

The house carried no indications of wealth but was comfortable enough. The kitchen table at which we sat was covered with a white lace cloth and there was a large statue of the Virgin Mary in the sitting room. The only other noteworthy feature was a cluster of crucifixes on the walls of the small entrance hall.

It was soon our turn to speak with Katya.

'Mike is a journalist,' said Ron, introducing me. 'And he would like to ask you some questions.' Ricardo translated, and Katya nodded and looked at me, waiting. I'd been told she would be expecting me to address her directly in English, which she spoke moderately well.

I was instantly annoyed at Ron for opening proceedings this way. I hadn't wanted to be introduced as a journalist – and I had no questions prepared to ask. It was premature. But I smiled warmly and tried not to let my irritation show as I cobbled together a couple of questions on the spot. I can't remember what I asked or how she answered, but I do recall that they were basic and fatuous questions, the kind someone who is on the spot and unprepared would ask. I felt quite frustrated by the less-than-ideal first impression I was making. We only spoke for a few minutes before it was clear we were done. I do recall Katya's final remark: 'Typical journalist,' she had said in Spanish, as we stood up to leave.

It was a poor start and I left Katya's house feeling flat and tired, probably from the long flight. I turned my thoughts to the next day. Another claim that Ron had relayed to me about Katya was that the Virgin Mary would sometimes appear to her and speak to her. My trip to Bolivia had been timed to coincide with one of these apparitions – and tomorrow was the day.

One of a number of odd things about the Virgin Mary claims was that Katya was able to pinpoint a date for the apparitions, and therefore invite people to attend and witness. A second oddity was that Katya seemed to know the specific location of the upcoming apparition – this time, it was to be deep in the jungle of the Chapare region of Bolivia, a number of hours' drive from where Katya lived in Cochabamba.

Ron, as usual, was undeterred by my scepticism. 'The Virgin Mary has told Katya that the next apparition will be her last and people have been invited to be present,' he had explained. I understood that the deal with the apparition was that, if true, it would only be seen by Katya, but I still wanted to be there when it happened. I was sure that if it was a set-up, the experience would somehow expose and incriminate the fraud behind it.

As I drifted off, I felt quietly confident that tomorrow would be the day things would begin to unravel. I slept deeply in the monastery hotel that night, my scepticism firmly intact.

Early the next morning we joined about 50 other people at a meeting point to travel in convoy to the region of Chapare where the apparition was supposed to take place. The first thing I observed was the lack of organisation. There was confusion and argument about who was to travel in what vehicle and there appeared to be no leadership. Katya stood quietly with a younger man, who I later found out was her son Francisco. She gave no direction and simply observed the chaos. I was introduced to a Father Renzo Sessolo, an Italian priest and Katya's spiritual advisor. I asked him what was happening and who was running the operation. He looked at the people and shrugged.

Finally, Ricardo took over. He bundled the foreigners – Ron and his wife, Gabrielle, five Americans and me – into a minibus.

'Just go,' he said to the driver, 'and I will get the others moving.'

That it was so poorly organised intrigued me. If it was fraud, it seemed there were very few people involved. And only one person had shown leadership – Ricardo, my number one suspect.

The drive to Chapare, which also happened to be the cocaine capitol of Bolivia, was downright frightening. The mountains were high and the valleys were deep; the road was eroded and potholed. We were constantly confronted by dangerously overloaded old trucks, driving on neither the left nor the right side of the road. Instead they stuck to whatever section of the road had the most bitumen, to the extent that we would need to pull into precarious shoulders to allow them to pass before we could proceed. Ron, who had done a stint driving trucks in the army, helpfully observed that the trucks appeared to be carrying up to three times their due weight and could not possibly rely on their brakes. We saw numerous sorry remnants of Ron's calculations. The whole experience was very hairy.

We eventually arrived, followed piece by piece by the rest of the convoy, at a roughly fenced field in a place called Candelaria. From the complete lack of vegetation and the amount of dung within the fenced area, I guessed the field had formerly held goats. After stretching my legs and decompressing from the road trip, I turned my attention to finding Katya.

Soon I saw that she was standing with Father Renzo, in front of a group of fir trees which stood outside the cleared field, on the side furthest from the road we had come in on. They appeared to be praying. A large group of about 70 to 80 people was forming behind her and around her, all looking in the same direction that Katya was, scouring the trees for something. I made my way over to the back of the crowd but hung back to observe properly.

'There she is!' a woman cried out. 'The Virgin!'

Others soon joined in: 'I can see her!' 'There she is!' 'I see her!'

Others rushed to join those who were pointing and shouting, 'Where?' 'Where?'

The voices were urgent, excited. Hysteria was taking hold. They were pointing in the direction of the trees. I walked around the crowd and towards the trees, then turned and faced the group of followers, where I began to film their reactions using a small single-chip video camera. While many were insisting they could see the apparition, they were all pointing in different directions. Katya and the priest played no part in this. It all felt absurd: many of these people seemed ready to believe anything. I pressed the Off button. This footage was worthless, other than perhaps to demonstrate the gullibility of crowds.

I wandered back away from the crowd and stood alone in the middle of the overgrazed goat paddock, feeling my solitude in both a physical and mental sense.

Suddenly, a burst of fragrance – the *same* fragrance I had smelt at Katya's home – hit me. I pressed the record button and swung the camera towards Katya. Just then, she fell without warning onto her knees, as if collapsing. Ron was in close, filming with his professional camera. I hurried to get closer. Katya was staring towards the trees and appeared to be in a state of ecstasy. I looked at the rest of those gathered: with the exception of the priest, they were all looking towards the trees, still searching for something. Katya's eyes were focused. Father Renzo was praying quietly, his eyes downcast and his lips moving swiftly. Why was he not looking? Did he know this vision was only for Katya? Or did he know there was nothing there?

And me? My complacency was shaken. When I first smelled the fragrance, I acknowledged it was unusual for any odour to come from no obvious place and to then disappear as abruptly as it arrived. Also, it was very attractive and appeared to be natural, not like a perfume. I also knew there could be many explanations. But how many explanations could there be for the *timing* of this second experience, I wondered. The appearance of fragrance had been followed immediately by Katya falling to the ground – and she had dropped in a very convincing manner. I had immediately thought that a good actress could do the same. But the timing intrigued me.

After a time, Katya turned and spoke to Father Renzo. He produced a notebook and pen. Katya returned her gaze and focus to a place in the trees and started speaking. Father Renzo took notes. I could see that this was meant to be the Virgin Mary talking to Katya, and Katya was repeating the words so that the priest could write them down. Katya seemed occasionally to be distracted and would look down at her hands. Father Renzo would then discreetly take a tissue from his pocket and hand it to her. She in turn would wipe her hands and pass it back to him.

The crowd had by now lost interest in their personal apparitions in the trees and were quietly focused on Katya, many of them having dropped to their knees to pray. And then it was over. The people gathered closer and Father Renzo read aloud, in Spanish, the words he had written. While he read, it gave me time to think. Had I just witnessed an apparition of the Virgin Mary to this woman, Katya Rivas? I had no idea.

Father Renzo finished reading, and the crowd began to disperse, back to the vehicles parked near the road. Ron had told me earlier that there was another 'mystic' attending the event – an American woman by the name of Nancy Fowler who also claimed to receive messages from the Virgin Mary and who had built quite a following of her own. He had pointed her out to me as the convoy arrived, and I had kept half an eye on her. During the event we had just witnessed, whatever it was, she had been part of the crowd searching the fir trees for visions. Now that the crowd had dispersed, however, she approached Katya. I made my way towards them and stood a few feet away as they talked.

'Are you sure she was there?' Fowler asked. 'I didn't see her. I didn't hear her. Maybe I've lost my grace.' Definitely not an accomplice, then, I thought. (I went to a later experience with her and found her totally unconvincing.)

Before we left the field and as we made our way back to the minibus, I noticed Father Renzo quietly passing a tissue from his pocket to Katya several more times. Each time she would wipe her hands before passing it back. Her face showed no sign of perspiration, nor had I seen her wipe her face.

Now that I could observe everyone's travel arrangements, I noted that Katya and her son Francisco were in the same car as Father Renzo. Ricardo, however, was in another. On our way back, the convoy stopped at a small church and everyone went in to pray. I knelt behind Katya, and at one point saw her look at her hands and then turn to Father Renzo who shook his head. It seemed he was out of tissues. I took a handkerchief from my pocket and reached forward and offered it to Katya. She nodded a small thanks, wiped her hands and handed it back to me. I retreated to a seat by the wall and then put the small piece of linen to my nose. It was the *same* fragrance. Beautiful, natural and distinctive. The cloth did not have the feeling of dampness you would expect from perspiration; in fact, I could detect nothing, apart from the smell. I had to admit, it chilled me. If this was a scam, which I knew it must be, it was fairly elegantly executed. I also had to admit that my curiosity was piqued. I stuffed my handkerchief back into my pocket and joined the others for the rest of the treacherous trip home.

Back in Cochabamba, I was invited to a party with Ron and Ricardo. Our hosts were a local well-to-do family. Their house was old, made of timber and creaking at the seams, but it was very charming, and the atmosphere was bright.

After a few introductions and small talk, I got talking with Katya's son Francisco, a good-looking man in his early thirties.

'I wanted to talk to you,' he said, 'because I also work in newspapers. I thought maybe we could see these things the same way.'

'What do you think of *these things*?' I asked, appreciating his choice of words.

'Well,' he said. 'When my mother said Jesus was talking to her, I wanted her to see a psychiatrist.' He was looking at me earnestly. 'If your mother said Jesus was talking to her, wouldn't you want her to see a psychiatrist?'

'And what do you think now?' I asked.

He held up one hand, as if to indicate that he was intending to explain. 'I am working and studying in Argentina at the moment,' he said, 'and every week I attend a rational group.'

'You are a rationalist?' I asked.

'Yes. We discuss matters and we argue, but always from a rational point of view.'

'Does that leave room for God?' I asked.

'No, it doesn't,' he said. 'From the point of logic, it doesn't.'

'So you can't believe your mother is a mystic?'

'Not really,' he said with a little hesitation, 'but let me tell you something. When we went to Chapare, I was in the same car as my mother, so I was with her the whole day. I don't think you could have noticed this, but oil was coming from her hands all day; she had to keep wiping it off. Now that is strange, but there's more to the story. It smells fantastic. This oil on her hands smells better than perfumes. How can you explain that?'

A moment of silence passed before I answered him.

'I can't explain it,' I admitted. *Not yet anyway*, I thought.

The party went smoothly and pleasantly, and I observed two things: Katya was given no special treatment and there were no outward signs of any special relationship between Katya and Ricardo. Back in my hotel room that night, in the old monastery, I took out the handkerchief and again put it to my nose – the fragrance was still there. I played over in my mind a number of scenarios for such a trick and some were quite plausible, but to have the hands leak oil all day was more difficult. And I could think of nothing that would explain my smelling the fragrance outside Katya's house and its sudden reappearance in the field immediately before Katya dropped to her knees. It seemed unfair. I had not come all this way to investigate something so nebulous. A fragrance in the air, with no apparent source, cannot be photographed, measured or analysed. And if a laboratory could show that the handkerchief contained a certain oil, a certain fragrance, then so what? It proved nothing.

Then there were the books, filled with words written in longhand by Katya. Or 'transcribed' by Katya, if we were to believe her. Katya's supporters repeatedly drew attention to the fact that she was uneducated and had not even read the Bible, let alone studied theology. This, they said, proved that these beautiful and profound writings were not in any way her creation. Her 'transcriptions' even included large slabs of quotes from the New and Old Testaments.

Despite being a non-believer, from the small amounts of these books that I read, I could see they were profound and brilliantly written. But my sceptical mind was still looking for fault – I was still asking myself who could have assisted her. Or was she a savant who could remember up to an hour of dictation and then repeat it faithfully? I knew that was unlikely, but it was possible. Some people can do extraordinary things with their minds.

I did not believe in the supernatural, so I was looking for other answers.

On one occasion, Ron filmed her writing non-stop with her pen barely leaving the paper for approximately an hour. I had to concede that no expert in any field was likely to be able to replicate that feat without having to stop and think of the next sentence or the next idea, or even just to make a correction. Ron had leafed through a number of her books – he attested that there were no corrections in any of them. All I was left with was the possibility that there was something supernatural in her brain that was bringing these incredible results.

But even then, how did I fit that into a visual story for television, even if I proved another source for her material? What did I do with that for television? Read from the book? Interview someone? Even when I looked at the positives that could be placed into this story, I still could not see a worthwhile story coming out of it.

But I had to admit, these experiences opened my mind a little. I could not deny that the fragrance and the writings had happened. But it all somehow seemed an impediment to clear thinking, as opposed to being clarifying. I wanted proof, one way or another, not confusion.

Eleven
Evidence

The next day Ricardo and Ron took me to see the bleeding statue of Cochabamba. On our way, Ricardo explained to me how he had come to be involved in this claim.

'A journalist called me about this phenomenon in April 1995. He had filmed it for local television and he knew I had been looking at these cases. I came here and it happened before my eyes. First it was clear, like tears, and then a large tear of liquid which looked like blood came from the left eye. It fell about six centimetres and I collected it as a specimen. There were seven witnesses: one caught it on video. So I called Ron and invited him to meet me in New Orleans. There was a laboratory there with a good reputation for DNA analysis.'

Ron took up the story. 'I filmed Ricardo handing over the sample and then we came back here to Cochabamba. We put the statue through a CAT scan at a laboratory here and they found no perforation, no hole. Nothing came from inside the statue. We took more samples and took them to two other laboratories in Sydney and Rome. Mike, all three laboratories said the samples passed the test for human blood, but not one could extract a DNA profile.'

He saw the question on my face but continued. 'We interviewed fifteen witnesses; all had seen either tears or blood.'

'You saw it too,' said Ricardo.

'Yes,' said Ron. 'I actually filmed the statue in close-up as it wept tears on two separate occasions over two days.'

They had a point, or maybe two points. Clearly something was happening with this statue that numerous people had witnessed. But was there fraud behind it? And could I uncover that fraud? I noted that it was again Ricardo who was a key player in the 'testing' which supported the claim. I was back to what I had feared when flying over: failure to prove fraud does not necessarily lead to finding truth.

When we arrived, I was again introduced to a number of people who were gathered at the statue and had to engage in some polite conversation before getting a chance to take a really good look.

The statue was unremarkable: a plaster bust, executed in a realist style, depicting the face of Jesus. In this one, Christ's tormented face had uncannily life-like eyes. The original sculpture, from which this one had been copied, was known as *The Crucifix of Limpias* after it reportedly shed tears of blood in a small Spanish village in 1919. Thousands of cheap plaster replicas had proliferated around the world.

Traditionally called the *Ecce Homo* image, the sculpture represents the moment in the Passion of Christ when He was brought back before the Roman Prefect of Judea, Pontius Pilate, after being brutalised by Roman soldiers. He held a reed in His hand in lieu of a sceptre and wore a 'crown' of roughly woven thorns on His head. He looked so wretched – bloodied by whips to which metal hooks had been attached – that the assembled crowd turned away, unable to look at Him, prompting Pontius Pilate to present Him to the mob with the mocking cry of, *'Ecce homo!'* – 'Behold the man!'.

The statue belonged to an airline hostess named Silvia Arevalo, who had bought it in Cochabamba on 11 March 1995. She brought it home and spent a few hours cleaning out a spare room which she'd been using as a gym. She wanted to turn it into a space for quiet contemplation of her faith. When she'd finished, she gathered her family to show them what she'd done and invited them to pray in front of it on the mantelpiece.

When her cousin came in, she asked who had been spraying water on the statue, before there was a sudden, shocked, realisation.

'This cannot be possible.'

They all claimed to have seen what they thought were tears running down the face of the statue.

Some years later, I asked Silvia's daughter, Kim Arevalo, what her reaction was when, as a 17-year-old, she first saw tears coming from the statue's eyes.

'I was somewhere between excited and scared,' the now middle-aged Kim said. 'My heart started beating really fast. I started sweating. I didn't know if I should laugh, if it was a good sign, if it was a bad sign. All I knew was I found myself on my knees and started crying myself.'

Two days later, a red substance had started coming from the statue's head.

'The first time I saw the statue bleed,' Kim told me, 'that's when I felt truly scared. I felt like God was warning us about something and I didn't know what it was.'

Over the course of the next year or so, more people saw the statue 'cry', while others saw 'blood' come out of its head.

Ron had already started investigating the statue two years

earlier, long before I got involved. When he first arrived at Silvia's house, he had seen what he thought might be the beginnings of tears forming in the statue's eyes, so he set up a camera on time lapse to watch it all night. It did cry and he captured it all on tape.

He and Ricardo Castanon then collected samples of the tears and the coagulated 'blood' and sent them to Professor Angelo Fiori of the Department of Legal Medicine, Gemelli University Hospital in Rome in Italy for analysis. Ron asked Fiori to analyse the material without telling the professor what it was that he was looking at.

In his report to Ron on 23 April 1998, Professor Fiori wrote: 'The new analysis performed on the bloodstains allowed only to confirm that the material examined is blood and that it has human origin. However, and surprisingly, the new DNA analysis were again completely negative, that is, no PCR amplification was obtained although the specimen is quite abundant. I have no explanation for this unusual phenomenon.'

Another lab gave a surprisingly descriptive account of their inability to find DNA on the sample: 'It's like saying we have the fact of it being a human hand and yet are unable to discern any fingerprints although we know that we should.'

Cochabamba's archbishop had already accepted the authenticity of this statue's suffering. When Ron had told me about all this in his early attempts to convince me of what was going on, I had dismissed it all. No matter what the evidence, I wasn't going to be swayed. My unwillingness to examine his evidence created a sense of resentment in Ron, but he was getting to have at least something of an I-told-you-so moment, as I came to walk in his investigative footsteps.

Now, as I looked at the statue closely, I could see that the face was streaked with what appeared to be dried blood.

Dark streaks flowed from the forehead down the contours of the statue's face. The statue had originally rolled off the production line with a few neatly painted-on drops of blood in the shape of teardrops – the sort of iconography that was not going to scare the children or put off those who might buy such things. But by now, it looked like the victim of a violent assault. There was an external layer of something like blackened blood around the forehead and cheeks and what looked like bruising around the eyes.

The upturned eyes and open mouth captured a man in enormous physical and emotional suffering. The face portrayed unfathomable sorrow. If this was fraud, it at least had artistic merit.

Alas, it did not turn on the tears for me that day, and again I left not knowing what to think.

Back at the old monastery, I sat alone in the rotunda and ordered a beer. The day was warm and the *cerveza* was cold. I thought through the events of the last few days – paying particular heed to the people I had met. You would have to say that someone who said that Jesus was giving her messages and that Mary was also appearing to her was seeking attention. But Katya Rivas did not behave like someone seeking attention. She didn't play to the cameras. She had followers but showed no sign of cultivating them. There was no sign of cult. There were no indications of money changing hands. The bleeding statue, inanimate but sad, was similarly low-key; no posters, no collection box. And it did not 'bleed' for me – a missed opportunity if it was a hoax.

There was the issue of the fragrance, but it occurred to me that if that was evidence then I had only had a sniff of it, and that thought made me laugh. And as for Ricardo being a suspect; again, I had nothing. The priest, Father Renzo Sessolo, seemed to be a decent, gentle, humble man who truly loved his God. There was nothing about him that suggested he could be a party to deceit. Both he and Katya seemed more interested in their prayer life than in trying to impress me.

I could only conclude that while there was some consensus that the events taking place in Bolivia had occurred in the way that Ron and Ricardo had reported them to me, I had seen nothing that proved them to be 'interventions' from God. Yes, there had been elements which I could not figure out, but my lack of evidence against them did not prove they were acts of God. While Katya and the other people I met appeared to be well-intentioned and not out to defraud others, this also didn't prove God's part in what was happening.

Ron was disappointed at my failure to respond to these things he believed in. But I did not see it as Ron had seen it. For me, it was simply a lack of evidence. And even if I had believed, as Ron did, I did not think any network would want to buy this story.

I was wrong.

Part Four

Finding the Story

Twelve

A Second Chance

I left Bolivia happy that I could put the whole subject behind me and get on with finishing *The Last Warriors*. Soon after returning to Sydney, though, I got a call from a television program called *Australian Story*, asking if I would agree to be the subject of one of their 30-minute documentaries. The program belonged to the ABC network and had an attractive format: one key interview with the subject, cut with observations from others. The interviewer's questions were deleted so the finished product was like a series of talking heads. It was well produced, well shot and a popular and well-respected program. I was more than happy to agree.

Australian Story tries to give viewers a feel for the person behind the public persona, and so when they heard about my trip to Bolivia, the producer asked for some footage, which Ron provided. When the program went to air in September 1998, my trip to Bolivia was mentioned, and I spoke briefly about it to the camera as part of the larger interview, but I didn't make a big deal out of it. The program was great and rated well, which to me was the only measure that ever mattered in television.

Three months later, I was at a Christmas party at the home of Vicki Jones, a former publicist at the Nine network where I had spent much of my career. We were all having a good time, with a lot of catching up and old stories re-told.

Just before midnight, however, Vicki called for attention and asked: 'Did you all see Mike on *Australian Story*?'

Most, it seemed, had not.

'Well, you should,' said Vicki, 'because it was a great program. But, no problem, I'm going to show it to you now.'

I was embarrassed. The guests, while mostly friends, were in a very jovial mood with a few drinks under their belts. It didn't seem like the right time to sit down to a television doco. But surprisingly, once Vicki set it up, everyone quietened down and took seats to start watching. I wasn't very comfortable with what was unfolding, but I didn't want to be a spoilsport either.

When it finished, people very kindly gave it a round of applause. I was touched.

The partying resumed and I relaxed again. Until my former colleague David Hill made a beeline for me. David was a former sports director at Nine who was by this time executive vice-president of Rupert Murdoch's Fox network in the United States. David had been a bit of a gun at Nine, who really had changed the way the world watches sport. Every time you watch cricket with cameras at both ends of the ground and close-ups from midwicket, you've got Hill to thank. Every American who sees a continuous score and clock on the screen when they're watching the NFL has Hill to thank, plus ice hockey's glowing puck. All his ideas. He was an innovator, full of creativity.

David pulled me aside. 'Did you really go all the way to Bolivia at your own expense to make those enquiries?' he asked.

I assured him that I had.

'You're an idiot,' he said, laughing. 'Journalists don't do things like that.'

David had an ability to laugh at most things. He had a very outgoing personality and a direct style, so I didn't feel like he was putting me down.

'Do you think there's anything in these crazy claims?' he asked.

'Yes, I do,' I said, without understanding why I was saying those words.

'Would you do an investigation for Fox? A Trans Media special?'

'Sure,' I said. It meant he'd have my company, Trans Media, employ the camera crews, producers, editors and researchers.

'Good,' he said. 'I'm going back to Los Angeles in a week. I'll call you early in the New Year.'

Driving home that night I asked myself why I had told David there might be something in the Bolivian claims when I'd told Ron the opposite. I don't lie and I don't make stories up. I am not the type to say something dishonest just to get a big commission — even for an American network. My positive response to David had just come out. It wasn't for reward or fame.

What I realised though was that I did want to go back to Bolivia. There was some pull there, some unfinished business. I felt a stir of excitement. Ron, I guessed, would feel more than a stir. I wondered how I'd tell him: 'You know how I said there was no story in Katya, well . . .'

But when I woke up the next morning, I began to doubt the seriousness of the conversation. I wondered if David had meant what he'd said about commissioning the show. Our deal had taken place in the wee hours of the morning, after a fair few drinks. I had to admit I'd gotten carried away myself, so

I hardly expected David to make good on his interest. *Lucky I hadn't already told Ron*, I thought as I dragged myself to the shower.

Then the phone rang. It was David.

'I haven't forgotten about your woman with the hotline to God,' he said. 'Do you still want to do it?'

I paused for a moment. Did I really want to go back? Did I truly think there was something there worth investigating properly?

I did. And there was.

David was delighted and full of ideas, so we chatted for a while about how the show might work.

As soon as I hung up, I called Ron. He took the news remarkably calmly, even cautiously.

'Do you think this guy will deliver on his offer? I mean, it was a late-night chat at a party,' he said.

'He says he still wants me to do it,' I said, 'but before I can make a commitment to him, I need to be satisfied about a number of matters of access to Katya and the statue and I will need permission to take blood samples. Most of all, I must be guaranteed that I will be able to film the stigmata: before, during and after.'

'That makes sense,' said Ron. 'I suggest we go back to Bolivia to sort this all out. Have a meeting with Katya, Father Renzo and Ricardo.'

'Well, let's get on a plane and go before he changes his mind,' I said.

Since the early 1990s, Ron had been driven by the desire to find out whether God is an interventionist God; does He interfere in the affairs of man?

For Ron, the journey had started in Gosford, an 80-kilometre drive north of Sydney. One day in mid-1987, a priest walked into his legal practice there without an appointment, wearing the full black cassock and dog collar like something out of Ron's Catholic childhood. Although Ron was raised a Catholic by his Italian-born parents, he ceased to practise his faith as a young adult.

You had to make an appointment to see Ron, but there was something indelible about his upbringing that stopped Ron from sending the priest packing. The priest, short and round and wearing wire-rimmed glasses, introduced himself as Father Bill Aliprandi, the recently appointed priest to the parish of Kincumber, a lakeside village about 10 kilometres east of Gosford.

Ron continues with the story in his book *Reason to Believe*. Father Aliprandi explained that the bishop had instructed him to build a church and a school for his sleepy backwater parish as its population was growing fast.

'But the parish is a poor one, and has no land,' Father Aliprandi explained. 'As for myself, I, err, well, I have no money either.'

'Well, how can I help you, Father?' Ron asked, feeling like he already knew the answer.

'I've found it,' the priest said.

'You've found the money?'

'Not the money. I've found the land. I walk past it every day and it's the right land. At the moment, it doesn't look like much; thick bush and there's only a small dirt track on the one side. But once it's cleared it'll be ideal because it's near the village.'

'Is it for sale?'

'No.'

'Do you know who owns it?'

'No, but I . . .'

'Let me get this straight. You don't have any money whatsoever. And you want to buy some land which is not for sale.'

'That's correct,' Father Aliprandi continued, apparently not picking up on Ron's contemptuous tone. 'But there's more. You see, every day I've been praying about this business of building a church and then I felt strongly that this was the right place for it, and so I walked on it and I made a cross with some stones and now every day I go there and I kneel on the ground and I pray to God that we might obtain it.'

Ron was stunned into silence by this dreamer's superstitious naivety. By his confidence in this nonsense. The priest continued on about how he'd enlisted the help of an influential woman.

'Who is she?' Ron asked.

'*Was*,' the priest laughed. 'Your question should be, "Who *was* she?" She's not quite with us, err, so to speak.'

The woman had died in 1909, he said. He was talking about Mary MacKillop, the nun who'd founded an order of teaching nuns, the Sisters of St Joseph of the Sacred Heart, and who had started an orphanage at South Kincumber a hundred years earlier in 1887. Father Aliprandi prattled on about how they were hoping MacKillop would be beatified soon, as Ron fidgeted with his pen, clearly bored.

'All I've done is nail a relic of hers to a tree on that land, and I'm praying for her intercession, so we can have it.'

Ron looked confused. 'A relic?'

'Oh, it's not much. Just a small snippet of one of the habits she used to wear.'

Wanting to ground the conversation in something a little more earthly, Ron pulled out a zoning map and the priest pointed to the block that he coveted. And Ron quickly deciphered the codes.

'Father, I'm sorry to disappoint you, but you'll never be able to build your church on this particular piece of property. City council regulations have it zoned as reserved for conservation and you're simply not allowed to build a church or a school on it.'

Ron was relieved. He wouldn't have to deal with this again. The priest stayed silent and dropped his gaze, and Ron would later suppose that it was a sense of pity for the poor man which led him to promise to see what he could do as he showed the priest to the door.

A few days later, Ron was in an appointment with a new client – a businessman, who was explaining that he needed to liquidate his company in a hurry and sell a block of land in the nearby seaside town of Terrigal. The land was valuable, and he already had a buyer lined up. That was all straightforward. But he had a second block of land that was going to be a lot harder to sell because it had no infrastructure servicing it. No roads, electricity, water or sewerage.

Ron pulled out his zoning map and rolled it out across the desk. The owner quickly found the block and put his finger on it. Ron sighed and slumped into his chair. It was, of course, Father Aliprandi's dream block.

The owner asked Ron what the problem was, but Ron assured him it was nothing. As Ron stared out the window, the owner had a moment to look at the map and noticed something wrong. Ron's map was out of date. The block had recently been rezoned residential, he explained. And that was a good thing, wasn't it?

As Ron would later describe it, he was listening, but the words were sliding by. And try as he might to refocus on the business at hand, he couldn't help thinking about that tree with a scrap of a dead nun's habit nailed to it.

The sale of the first block of land proceeded quickly, with a buyer agreeing to purchase it for a couple of million dollars. But when the time came to sign the paperwork, the landowner suddenly decided to increase the price by $200,000. There was a serious disagreement and the buyer was about to walk. Ron did some fancy footwork and pointed out an obscure loophole in the planning regulations which made the block worth a lot more than anyone had previously realised. But it wasn't enough. The buyer walked away.

Somewhat deflated, Ron took the landowner out to lunch where he had Father Aliprandi waiting for them at the restaurant. Aliprandi explained the situation and Ron was shocked when the owner, having just inflated the price of one block, massively deflated the price of the other to offer it to the priest for just $210,000.

It was a steal, but Father Aliprandi reminded the businessman and Ron that he still didn't have any money.

'Look,' the landowner responded, 'I'll sell you an option on the land for a dollar.'

Father Aliprandi fumbled in his pockets but only came up with 80 cents.

'I owe you twenty cents.'

'Done.'

They all laughed and shook hands.

Father Aliprandi turned to the owner: 'For such an act of commitment to God, don't be surprised if you're blessed by God and good things happen to you. Even today.'

They didn't have to wait long. Back in Ron's office after lunch, the buyer who'd walked out hours earlier walked back in. He'd checked out what Ron had said about the loophole and it was right. The deal was signed then and there on what was for Ron, a very memorable Friday.

The following Tuesday morning, Ron was in the office early, before anyone else had arrived, when the landowner rang him, exultant. Stock markets around the globe had crashed overnight and Australia was set to follow suit. Billions were being wiped clean off the world's investment portfolios and he was absolutely stoked.

'I would never be able to get the same price for my land today as I got last Friday. It's like winning the lottery. How lucky is that!'

Ron had to wonder.

A few months later, the priest was still battling to raise the outstanding $209,999.20 when another piece of 'luck' went his way. The state government announced it was going to build a new high school right next to the block the priest had optioned. Suddenly, all that infrastructure was about to be delivered – for free.

As a result, the land was now worth an awful lot more than it had been when the deal was made. But there was only ever a verbal agreement to sell it, so Ron knew the owner could easily slide away from it. But he didn't. Father Aliprandi and the Church came up with the money and the deal eventually went through.

Ron could not quite believe the sequence of events that he'd witnessed over just a few months. He later asked Father Aliprandi about it – whether he really believed when he knelt down to pray for that land that he would actually get it.

'I had no doubt,' the priest said. 'I've set aside my life to work for God and I asked Him for His help . . . I would have been surprised if He had *not* helped me.'

Holy Cross Catholic Primary School, Kincumber, opened in 1991 with 50 students and the only person not surprised was Father Bill Aliprandi.

Ron, meanwhile, had started questioning his own system of beliefs. He began to think that the priest had walked into his office for a reason — that he was supposed to see and be involved in the events which had played out. He described it as a door being opened and him feeling compelled to peer through it.

Since then, he'd well and truly walked through that door, and now he was trying to drag me and the rest of the world through it with him.

Thirteen

The Start of Something

It was 14 January 1999 when Ron and I landed in Buenos Aires, Argentina, and headed to the airline check-in counter to get boarding passes for the flight to Bolivia. The terminal was hot and crowded, and it seemed about a thousand passengers were trying to do the same thing at the same time. The lines were untidy and there was some jostling. We were both tired and I was distracted, trying to work out the quickest way through this transfer. I was a seasoned traveller and could usually navigate airports pretty easily.

For international travel, I always carried a special wallet for tickets, passport, credit cards and a lot of cash – US$15,000 on this occasion. My special wallet was in the outer pouch of my backpack. As I stood there amid the throng, I felt a tug on my backpack and looked around. There was a woman in her early forties standing there. I felt a second tug and swung around to see the back of the same woman being swallowed up by the crowd. The outer pouch of the backpack was open and the wallet was gone.

I experienced an enormous sinking feeling as the realisation hit home that everything we'd planned – our meeting with Katya, the possibility of a documentary with Fox – was now seriously under threat. And in that instant, I knew how important this meeting in Bolivia had become to me, and how gutted I would be if we had to forfeit our mission.

I turned to Ron, 'We're not getting on this plane. My wallet's been stolen.'

The immediate panic on his face reflected my own.

'Did you see who took it?'

'Yes,' I said. 'It was a woman. Blonde.'

'Can we find her?'

'I doubt it,' I said, 'and even if we could, she won't have it on her. I'm sure she's a pro. She will have passed it to someone else.'

'Mike, we've got to try.'

'This room's got a thousand people in it,' I said, becoming more agitated by the second. 'If I grab her and call the police, she'll call the police and tell them I am molesting her or something. There's no way out. We won't make that meeting.'

The airport buzz seemed to go quiet. I felt very far away for a moment, almost like I was in a dream sequence. Three words burst out of me from somewhere deep: 'Jesus, not now!'

What I meant by that utterance was that I accepted that when I go through hundreds of foreign airports I'll get robbed eventually. But not now. Somehow, I understood that Jesus would know what I was saying. Yet I didn't think that Jesus existed. It was a turning point.

Ron was still at me, asking those sensible lawyer questions. 'What'd she look like? Can you give me a description? Let's find her.'

I looked over his shoulder and could barely believe what I saw. The blonde woman was pushing her way back through

Finding the Story

the crowd towards me. As she got closer, I could see she was holding my wallet. She approached me directly and pushed the wallet into my hands. I took it silently, not quite comprehending what I was experiencing. She turned and disappeared as quickly as when she had taken it. Nobody spoke.

Ron was the first to recover. 'Check it! Quickly, check it. Is the cash there?'

'I don't need to check it,' I said serenely. 'The money's all there.'

I just knew it. But, of course, I did open the wallet and in one glance I could see the airline tickets and a thick wad of green $100 bills. I felt an immediate and immense sense of relief, but at the same time I felt a much stronger emotion overwhelming me. Something extraordinary had just happened and I needed time to digest it.

A thief from a poor country had just stolen a small fortune and voluntarily returned it. That was extraordinary. But to me something even stranger had happened. Those three words: 'Jesus, not now.' I had not used them in despair, nor anger. It had not been a blasphemous exclamation. *It had been a prayer.*

But why I would have offered a prayer at that moment eluded me – such a reaction was foreign to me. Aside from that moment in the plane in Africa, I hadn't prayed since my early teens. There was no god in my life. It seemed to me that those three words belonged only to someone who believed in God and accepted that this heavenly being would hear your prayers and answer them. I had no right to use those words. But my wallet had been returned. And when I thought about it, I realised that I hadn't prayed for the money to be returned: what I really wanted was what was necessary to get on the plane and attend the meeting with Katya.

As we completed our transfer and I boarded the plane, I was silent. I was thinking about that other aircraft in Africa . . . and that other prayer, almost a year earlier. I spent the whole plane trip pondering what it all meant. Pondering who I was working for. Was I doing this for Fox, or a god I didn't even believe in?

Within a few days, I knew that I would go ahead and film my investigations for the Fox network. Returning to Bolivia as a television producer and reporter, I was much more comfortable than I had been the first time around when I didn't quite know what role to play. This time around, I knew exactly what to scope out and what issues I needed to resolve. What could I film? Who should I interview? My work was tangible, even if the answers were not.

Ron now assumed the role of a valuable repository of research. He had been following what was now *my* story for four or five years. He had video footage of the statue of Christ bleeding. Sure, that was not proof, but for television reporting, when you talk about something, you need pictures.

The meeting in Bolivia became a series of meetings as we tried to figure out what we could do and how we could do it. As time went on, Katya became more open with me. She could not promise I would see the stigmata, but she said that if it did happen, I would have full access with my cameras – before, during and after. The rest, she intimated, would be in the hands of the Lord.

I kept finding myself circling back to one central question for which there seemed no answer. If all this stuff was real, what did God achieve by selecting somebody every hundred years or so and talking with them, giving them messages, and putting them through the stigmata? How did God choose these people? Why Bolivia? Why Katya? What was the result supposed to be?

To even begin to answer these questions, I realised that I needed to go back to brass tacks and do some extensive research.

The first place to start was with Bolivia itself. So many people in different countries have had their lands and cultures ravaged by war and death, have been subject to despots and dictators, and have suffered through extreme poverty and hunger. It shapes the way people think.

Bolivia was no exception.

The first thing that struck me in my research was that Bolivia is a physically stunning country – from the snowy heights of the Andes to the tropical rainforests. Once the home of the Aymara people whose spiritual place was Lake Titicaca, by the 15th century Bolivia had been conquered by the Incas. Indeed, the Inca language, Quechua, remains the dominant Indigenous language today.

You might imagine that in times when armies moved by foot, Bolivia would have been a difficult place to invade. But when the Spanish conquistadors came to this region in the 16th century, almost 500 years ago, they brought with them a weapon which was greater than the difficulties. That weapon was greed.

The resources they were greedy for were silver and gold, and the Spanish quest for them was a death sentence for millions. The Spaniards tracked the source of these precious metals with genocidal fervour, slaughtering all who stood in their path. The survivors and their descendants became labourers in the mines. It was bloodshed and exploitation in the extreme.

In the centuries to come, there would be more bloodshed, but the violence of the Spanish invasion would never be surpassed. The legacy of exploitation, however, would prove to be the running sore.

The nation's independence was also only achieved through a hard-won war. Simon Bolivar led Bolivia to independence in 1825 after a protracted 16-year struggle that devastated the country. And ultimately the flowering of the new Republic of Bolivia brought little change; for ordinary Bolivian people, it was the same old blossoms with new names. Those new leaders were the *caudillos*: military dictators who fought relentlessly for power and the spoils of office. The squabbling was endless – there would be a staggering 192 coups over the next 156 years.

The 20th century started with another civil war in which the north defeated the south, but it wasn't a matter of geography or even territory. The south was home to the silver mines of Potosi, and in the north, a group known as the 'new entrepreneurs' had formed. It was a war with a very familiar theme: the country's natural resources.

The 20th century also saw Bolivia's first elections but out of a population of some 4 million, less than 10,000 families voted. The native Aymara people were still treated as serfs – there was no possibility of the Indigenous peoples being allowed to vote, and they made up almost 90 per cent of the population. Technically, this was not ethnic discrimination. To qualify for the vote, you had to be a male who owned land and could read and write. In any case, this was all irrelevant to the question of government. The coups and the military dictators continued without impediment.

Finally, under the darkest of disguises, came the catalyst for much-needed change: the Chaco War. By 1932, oil had been discovered by an American company in the Bolivian region bordering Paraguay. This oil was attractive to Paraguay and even more attractive to other major oil companies. Paraguay, with the financial support of competing oil companies, invaded Bolivia's Gran Chaco region. It was a terrible war with Bolivia's death toll reaching 50,000 over three years. Bolivia also lost considerable territory and oil reserves.

But something happened to Bolivia during that terrible time. It was not dramatic nor immediately evident, but it was the start of something. For the first time, the native Aymara people were conscripted to fight. Young aristocratic officers found themselves fighting alongside the 'serfs'. In the trenches, relations between the two classes started to change in a manner which would prove cathartic to the nation.

The years after the Chaco War saw a gap developing between the emerging social conscience of the young officers and the oligarchy of the generals and three British tin miners, who were by then on the scene. Tin had replaced silver as the country's major source of wealth and contributed 70 per cent of the country's export earnings. The mines were in the hands of three British companies and, of course, were worked with cheap labour.

Capturing the mood for change, a new political party was formed. The Movimiento Nacional Revolucionario, the MNR, was held together by a great name in Bolivian politics, Víctor Paz Estenssoro, who was to go on to hold the presidency in the '50s, the '60s and the '80s. In true Bolivian tradition, his periods of power were interrupted by coups and exile.

In the strangest of elections in 1951, the MNR, with no candidates and no campaign, won government by 100,000 votes to 40,000. It was a hollow victory, however, which was followed by another coup d'état leading to a military dictatorship which presided over a period of great turmoil, with imprisonments and torture.

This battle, which was now generational, exploded in a short but bloody revolution in April 1952. The MNR, the police and a renegade interior minister from within the government combined forces and distributed arms to the people, including mine workers. Ordinary civilians fought in the streets of the capital, La Paz, and in the mining city of Oruro. After three days, eight military regiments had defected. It was all over.

The new president – Hernán Siles Zuazo – was flown back by air force pilot René Barrientos to a hero's reception and the MNR, with the unions, was now firmly in control. The mines were nationalised, the vast Indigenous population was given the vote and there was land reform. Land now belonged to those who worked it. Mine production doubled and workers were paid bonuses. It was a period of euphoria. The spirit born in the Chaco War had triumphed and emphatically changed the country.

It was the birth of modern Bolivia, Katya Rivas's home.

Fourteen

Katya's Story

As with almost all Bolivians, Katya's own personal story is inextricably linked to the fluctuating state of Bolivian politics, and the impact the country's history had on Bolivian people.

However, Katya's story was far from ordinary. The comfortable but basic house she lived in, her plain clothes and her unassuming nature gave no indication of the almost unbelievable life she had lived.

Katya's father was a political and military man. When the MNR had formed in the 1940s, Toro Rivas had been one of the young officers making up the strength of the movement. Toro made some powerful friends, some of whom became close to the family. Among them was the highly respected air force pilot René Barrientos, who had not only been at the centre of the MNR's victory in the early '50s, which was the catalyst for the transformation of the lives of Bolivian the people, but who would also go on to become the president of Bolivia in 1964.

Katya had known Barrientos for as long as she could remember. He was like an uncle or a *compadre* (godfather) to her and would take her to school and oversee her progress when her own father was absent on military or political matters. Katya and Barrientos enjoyed a close relationship, and she always enjoyed their discussions.

It was also through her father's connections that Katya Rivas met Tinino Rico Toro at an army party in 1960. Katya was 15, and Tinino was 24 and had just graduated from officers' school. Katya, by the consensus of all those I interviewed, was attractive, lively and the centre of attention.

That night, when Tinino asked her for a dance, she flirtatiously rejected him, pointing out that he brought a girlfriend with him. He responded by taking his girlfriend home and returning to the dance alone.

'Now will you dance with me?' he asked.

'Yes,' she said.

'He was not so handsome,' Katya recalled, 'but he was attractive. He danced very well, and he knew how to make a girl feel good.'

Katya and Tinino started seeing each other secretly, often after Mass. Katya's father was Tinino's general and Tinino was afraid of him, with good reason. By this time, Toro Rivas had been appointed to the position of Bolivian minister of security, which made him the right-hand man of the president.

The blossoming relationship between Katya and Tinino was straight out of a romance book. They were swept up in each other. Katya dropped out of sight from her usual friends and was no longer seen at the parties of the younger set. Within months, the couple had agreed to be married. When 15-year-old Katya told her parents, General Toro Rivas was furious.

'You will not marry him,' he said. 'He is not a good man; I have seen him beat his men. And besides, you are only 15. You are far too young to make this decision, and to make it so quickly.'

Finding the Story

Unfortunately, General Toro Rivas had a serious weakness in this argument: he himself had a mistress who was only 18 years of age. Katya's *compadre* General René Barrientos also tried to intervene to protect Katya and deter her from the marriage, but she was a strong-minded girl and was determined to marry her love.

Katya and Tinino Rico Toro were married in the spring of 1960, just weeks before her sixteenth birthday. It was common in Bolivia in those times for a girl to marry young, but not that young. And in the canon law of the Catholic Church – and 95 per cent of Bolivians were Catholic – it was not acceptable. But married they were.

They moved from Cochabamba to live in an army barracks in a small town in the north of Bolivia. The house was small, unattractive and lonely. Tinino was often absent and Katya had left her friends and family behind. None of the houses had telephones and calls would have to be made and taken from an office in the army barracks.

One day, in about the seventh month of their marriage, Katya was called to the telephone.

'I spoke with a lady who wanted to talk with Tinino,' Katya recalled, 'and it was clear to me that she had a relationship with him. I knew then that he was cheating on me. I did not know what to do. I just felt so sad. I knew my father had been right. My father had told me he feared he would be cruel to me as he was with his men.'

It was the start of a five-year sadness.

'He was very controlling, and he wanted me to have a schedule; to do everything on schedule. When I was expecting my first child, Tatiana, I had low blood pressure and my health was poor; I needed to rest and sleep. But he didn't like that.'

Tatiana's birth when Katya was just 17 years old involved complications that put Katya's life at risk. When doctors and medical staff warned Tinino that the situation was critical, he had been adamant: 'This will be a natural birth. There will be no surgery.'

'Your wife is suffering from pre-eclampsia,' the doctor explained. 'She is dying, and the baby is suffering.'

Eventually, Katya's mother intervened vehemently, and Tinino relented and authorised an emergency caesarean section to be performed. Tatiana was born on 28 January 1962.

'Not long after the birth of my daughter, my parents had to leave Bolivia for Argentina, so I was left now with only Tinino and little Tatiana,' Katya told me. 'At night, when my daughter cried, Tinino would not allow me to hold her – he insisted that the baby had to learn to survive without comfort.

'I had to sleep just holding my daughter's hand. I would push the cradle with my feet, so I could stop her crying without him noticing. So I cried and my daughter cried.'

Her second pregnancy to Tinino followed a similar path.

'This birth will be natural,' Tinino ordered as they approached the due date. 'You have had one with surgery. This one will be natural. I want many children.'

Katya went into labour, but it was not straightforward. The pushing, the breathing . . . the pushing, the breathing, the pain, went on and on. But the baby would not come. They waited and waited . . . and waited.

Again, the doctor faced Tinino and said: 'Sir, your wife and baby are dying.'

The young military officer relented. 'All right then, surgery.'

Katya looked at me calmly as she recalled what then took place.

'The baby died,' she said. 'A boy.'

Then with a surprising lack of bitterness, she added: 'The baby died because of him.' She was silent for a moment and her eyes became moist. 'They did not tell me for five days.'

'I was very much in pain because they didn't let me meet my baby. I didn't know my baby. I was also very sick. I had a kidney infection. They told me I could not see the baby because he was in an incubator. I asked why I could not go and see him in the incubator. They said because I was not well enough.'

Tatiana, who was translating for me, was very distressed by this story, and broke from the interview to speak in Spanish with Katya. Her need to understand this story was greater than mine.

After a time, Tatiana explained to me: 'The decision to keep the baby's death a secret was made by my father and the doctor. They called my grandparents and asked them to come. They explained that my mother was too sick to be told, so then everybody was involved in the lie.'

The news of the death of her son shattered Katya and she suffered grief and sadness for several years; her torment aggravated by her belief that her marriage could not be saved.

'It was only a few days later that I found he was cheating on me again. He had an affair. When I tried to talk to him about it, he told me I was crazy – that this "thing" [the death of her son] had affected me.'

He threatened to send her away to an insane asylum. Of course, she instead chose to turn a blind eye to her husband's infidelity, and to not challenge him in any way. Katya's grief, however, would stay with her for many more years. Her health declined due to the ongoing kidney infection and eventually, she had to have a transplant in Argentina.

It was only the birth of her third child – a son, Francisco – in August 1965 which finally pulled her out of her grief. With the arrival of Francisco, Katya's life improved. 'I found my whole world was filled with the two children.'

It was little more than a year into this period of Katya's life when the Marxist revolutionary Che Guevara entered Bolivia in November 1966. His presence was reportedly at the behest of the Cuban dictator, Fidel Castro, though there is reason to suspect that Guevara had actually gone rogue and was not acting on Castro's orders at all but was instead seeking an opportunity to prove his heroism after a string of failures.

At the time Guevara entered Bolivia, Katya's protective *compadre*, René Barrientos, was president of Bolivia. It wasn't long before reports of Guevara and his band of about 30 Cuban guerrillas were rumoured to have infiltrated Barrientos's government with spies – one of whom had supposedly become the president's lover. Guevara and his gang established a camp in the rural south-east and set about planning a revolution. As a distinguished and loyal member of the MNR, Katya's husband – now Captain Tinino Rico Toro – requested to lead the fight against the guerrillas. He got his wish.

Katya's marriage, however, had not improved, and Katya could see no way out. As the wife of Captain Tinino Rico Toro, Katya was well known to the troops of his Trinidad Company: they were mostly young conscripts, poorly trained and poorly paid. While Tinino was away fighting Che Guevara's rebels in the jungle, in the remote region around the Nancahuasu river, Katya was dreading his return. She knew the marriage could not continue, but she didn't know how she could end it. She even prayed that Tinino might die on the battlefield.

'Then one day I found a letter from him to a woman – another affair. He had sent it from the jungle. That was too much for me.'

Katya called on her old *compadre*, René Barrientos, for assistance.

It wasn't the first time Katya had used her family connection to the president to make things happen. Katya's brother, Ricardo (Richie) Rivas, who was also an army officer at the time, recounted to me what transpired between Katya and Barrientos the first time she decided to intercede.

'There were five Bolivian soldiers wounded but they could not be taken out of the jungle. Katya heard of this emergency on radio news reports and was angry that no helicopter could be made available. There were only three helicopters available to the army and Katya was told that one was used by some officers for a barbecue.

'She talked directly with the president, General René Barrientos, and asked how he could allow a helicopter to be at a picnic when some of these men were dying. The president then sent a helicopter to evacuate the seriously wounded to Santa Cruz and told Katya she must go to Santa Cruz to take responsibility for their medical care, which she did.

'She then flew with the two critical cases to the military hospital of La Paz. For this initiative and the work she later did with the wounded soldiers, she would become known as the "Angel of Nancahuasu",' Richie told me.

When I put this story to Katya, she played it down. 'Yes, I was angry that a helicopter could be at a picnic when men were dying. I called René and he agreed to send his helicopter, but he made it a condition that I take responsibility for the treatment and care of the wounded. The authority I was given was such that I was able to send one man to Panama for surgery.

'But I don't think the "Angel of Nancahuasu" story came from the men; it was just something the president said when he saw me at the hospital in La Paz. He talked like that.'

I asked Katya's son Francisco if he had heard this story.

'No,' he said, 'but it reminds me of something I had forgotten. When I was a boy, I was walking down the street one time with my mother when a man from the other side of the road saw her and started running towards her. He was shouting, "Mama! Mama!" and he hugged her and made a big fuss of her. I asked my mother what was happening, why was this man calling her Mama? She said, "Oh, he was one of the wounded soldiers I took care of."'

Second time around, Katya's direct access to the president was not as effective as she had hoped. Meeting with Barrientos in the presidential palace, she showed him the letter she had found from Tinino to his lover and asked for his support to divorce Tinino.

But Barrientos had a conflict of interest. He was concerned that a notice of divorce proceedings would distract Captain Tinino Rico Toro from the fight with Che Guevara and cause him to make poor military decisions. He pleaded with Katya to wait. Without her *compadre*'s support, Katya had no choice but to abandon her divorce plans until after the battle was done.

In September 1967, Captain Tinino Rico Toro's Trinidad Company fought the first full frontal battle with Guevara resulting in many deaths on both sides. Importantly, Guevara's supplies were discovered and seized, including the medicine for his chronic asthma.

On paper, Bolivia had appeared to provide Guevara with the perfect opportunity for a great victory. It had been an oppressed and poverty-stricken country. But Guevara seemed not to have understood the enormous attitude change from the Chaco War and the legislation that followed the revolution of 1952. The Aymara people now had the vote and their own land. Guevara had imagined the peasants flocking to join him. Instead, his revolution fizzled into an annihilation that would see him captured and executed.

Life after Che was good for René Barrientos. There is no doubting his popularity. He successfully courted the Aymara people and he spoke the dominant Quechua language; but it was his flamboyance that put the cream on his constituents' cake. It was never held against him in this Catholic country that he was a bigamist and womaniser.

Life after Che also changed drastically for Katya. She took the children and went to live with her mother in La Paz, and immediately commenced divorce proceedings.

For a brief time, she experienced a sense of freedom. However, she soon began to feel that freedom come under threat from an unlikely source: her *compadre*, President René Barrientos.

He started sending her chocolates and flowers. There was a radio program, 'The Listeners' Discotheque', hosted by a disc jockey named Lucho. Barrientos would call the program after midnight and ask for songs 'from René to Katya'.

Most embarrassing was an incident at the house of a friend of Katya's, Betty Eterovic. Betty had a big pool and invited friends and neighbours to use it. One day, Katya and a number of others were at the pool when the presidential helicopter arrived, flying in low and hovering over the pool. Roses were dropped from the cockpit as towels and umbrellas were blasted about the yard from above.

He was charming and flamboyant, and declared to Katya that he would leave his second wife for her. Katya was 24. He was 49. But it was not just the age factor that deterred Katya from responding to his advances, it was that she saw him as an uncle. To her, he was family. Katya was as polite as she could be, but she did not respond to his advances or give him any reason to think she would be in a relationship with him.

Barrientos's hard edge was also present in his pursuit of her. He had Katya's passport marked so that she could not leave the country and an army officer who had been courting her was suddenly dispatched to Santa Cruz, 500 kilometres to the east.

Barrientos would arrive unannounced at her mother's home and Katya would sometimes hide to avoid him. He would bring lollies for her children and spend time playing with them. On at least one occasion, he took Francisco for a ride in an aircraft. While Katya refused to meet with Barrientos privately, she accepted some gifts of jewellery.

And then there was the green dress. After another rejection by Katya, Barrientos had informed her that as she was to be First Lady one day, he had arranged for her official portrait to be painted by the artist Ato Garcia. Katya reluctantly agreed, and Barrientos bought her an expensive green dress to wear for the sittings, which she did on several occasions.

Despite this, Katya believed that time was on her side.

'He wants me more because he can't have me,' she told her mother. 'He is accustomed to getting any woman he wants. But soon he will see others he wants, and he will forget about me.'

Ironically, Katya sought to regain her freedom by agreeing to become engaged to the young officer who was courting her, but she didn't foresee what this would trigger in Barrientos. He immediately flew to Cochabamba to speak to her father, his old friend, about marrying Katya, but was again rebuffed.

'I would rather see her dead than married to you,' her father said.

Barrientos then wrote two letters to her mother. Katya was shocked by the contents of the first, and when the second letter arrived, she asked her mother about its content.

'I don't know what's happening,' her mother said. 'He's crazy and he says he is coming tonight.'

He did come that night and Katya's mother served tea. Katya noted that both of them appeared nervous, which was unusual for Barrientos.

'What's your problem?' Katya asked him.

'I have said all I have to say in the letter,' he replied, but then added: 'You need a protector.'

Katya's mother dropped a teacup.

On the morning of 27 March 1969, Katya was preparing to fly from La Paz to Santa Cruz to discuss her marriage plans with her fiancé.

She was working as a secretary in a mining company and had taken time off for this assignment. She dressed in a green sweater and slacks and went to the mirror for one last check. Her dark hair was cut close in the style of the American actress Audrey Hepburn. She gave it a push and prod and seemed satisfied.

A car pulled up outside the house and Katya looked through the window.

'Oh no. Not now. Not today.'

She found herself at the front door, opening it, heart racing and daring to hope there would be a simple explanation.

There were three men – one approaching the house, one behind and one standing near the car. Two were officers, smart in their military uniform. She knew all three.

'The president needs you urgently,' said the first young officer, gently.

'No, I'm in a hurry,' said Katya. 'I have to catch a plane at eleven.'

'I'm sorry, Katya, but you have to come. You know what he's like.'

The young man was clearly uncomfortable and looked away. Then, making eye contact, he completed his message: 'And you must wear the green dress.'

'I am already wearing green,' she said, coldly.

'You know the one,' he said, 'The formal green dress.'

Katya protested some more, but the three men stood their ground. They had their orders and the choice was not theirs. Katya knew that, and she too knew she had no choice.

She turned silently and went back into the house. Minutes later she returned without having changed into the formal outfit, carrying a handbag. The men looked at her, and then at each other, but said nothing. The first of the officers shrugged, and they walked her to the car. They drove, not to the presidential palace, but to the president's apartment where he had his second office.

As she walked into the apartment, Katya gasped at what was spread before her.

President René Barrientos was seated in a formal manner behind his desk wearing the ceremonial military uniform of a general, complete with a line of medals across his breast. Standing by were security officers, staff and a group of about 12 people, formally dressed. Katya recognised most of them; some were friends. Among them was her mother, at the sight of whom she felt a surge of anger.

'Why are you not wearing the green dress?' the president asked.

'Why should I?' she answered, and then with anger spilling, she turned to her mother. 'Mum, what are you doing here?' But her mother did not reply.

The president stood, walked to the door, and locked it. It

was a threatening act amid a scene of discomfort and intimidation, but for some reason Katya's first thought was that she would miss her plane. Katya stood there, alone. Barrientos was organising the people in the room and her mother appeared to be assisting. Barrientos and Katya's mother then led her to a side room and closed the door.

'I know why you are going to Santa Cruz,' said the president, 'but you will not leave here until we are married.'

'That's impossible,' she said. 'You're crazy.'

He told her that one of the people present was a marriage notary.

'No-one will leave this apartment until we are married,' he repeated.

'Let me think about it, please. I just need a little time,' she pleaded. 'I promise I will come back.'

'I am not a fool,' he replied.

'Then I shall just sit it out,' she said.

Barrientos walked back into the main room and addressed the 'wedding' guests.

'Let's eat and drink,' he said. 'Nobody can leave until she decides.'

He then went back to his desk and calmly resumed his presidential duties, reading and signing papers.

Katya was furious at her mother and confronted her. Her mother tried to excuse herself. 'I was ambushed,' she said.

Katya sat down angrily. She knew she had missed the plane to Santa Cruz, and she began to cry.

Katya knew the guests on the other side of the door would be blaming her. She only had to say 'yes', and they would soon be free to leave. And why should she say 'no'? She was only a secretary with two children and no money. Was it not a privilege to marry the president?

One of the security officers, who she knew as a friend, came to her side: 'Katya,' he said gently, 'you know him. You know he won't give up. You must . . . And please smile.'

Yes, he is crazy, she thought. *It will pass.*

The hours ticked by and the pressure finally got to her. She stood and strode to the book of marriage registrations. As she was signing, she was thinking of what she would say to the young man in Santa Cruz.

The president, as if reading her mind, said: 'I have changed your flight to 3 pm.' He said it warmly, sounding almost like the old René.

It was the 27th day of March 1969.

She caught the later flight to Santa Cruz to meet the young man who was expecting her hand in marriage, but even in this sad meeting, her thoughts were troubled beyond the obvious. In truth, she was not in love with her fiancé either.

She spent three miserable days in Santa Cruz and a further week in her home city of Cochabamba with her father in an attempt to avoid the president in La Paz. It helped that Barrientos had political problems and was travelling constantly, but he telephoned her every night. He had her signature on the marriage certificate, but he was still courting her. Their early conversations were strained and repetitive.

'I need time,' she would say. 'I am unhappy with the way you forced me to marry you.'

'Trust me,' he would say, 'I love you.'

Katya had to concede that she had not done herself any favours by accepting his presents, including the dress, and by sitting for the 'First Lady' portrait. She also told him that she was not qualified to be the wife of the president; that she lacked knowledge. She returned to her mother's house in La Paz and went back to her job with the mining company.

'I felt like I was living in a dream,' she recalled, 'and I couldn't find any way out. I kept thinking he must find somebody else. I thought God may help me.'

Incredibly, the marriage remained secret from the public, despite the number of witnesses, though rumours were seeping out. On one occasion, Katya was at the hairdresser and heard women gossiping about the president's new marriage. One woman said she had heard it was an Asian princess. Katya was pleased with the secrecy, but not that her name was now among those said to be having an affair with the president.

By the third week of their daily phone calls, Barrientos was becoming more understanding of Katya's situation and their relationship improved. One day she saw him in public and he stopped his car. She accepted his offer of a ride and was driven to her office with sirens sounding. They held hands. After that they had several clandestine meetings. He would wait for her in a small, non-presidential car, wearing a hat for disguise. They would sit and talk; his security squad parked nearby. Katya started to feel sympathy for him, he was troubled and tired.

'I feel at peace when I am with you,' he told her.

When he drove her home, there would be more security men waiting. In response to her concern that she was inadequate to be the wife of a president, she had a tutor instruct her in such matters as protocol and Bolivian history. Katya described this as 'First Lady' lessons.

On 26 April, Barrientos was flying out of La Paz and asked Katya to meet him at the airport. As a security officer drove her up the steep, winding climb to the airport, Katya felt uncomfortable. She would later describe the feeling as a premonition. When she met with Barrientos at the airport, the feeling persisted.

'I want you to come with me to Cochabamba,' he said.

'No, I can't,' she replied.

'And then we can fly to Santa Cruz,' he said. 'There is a house I want to show you.'

Katya knew where the conversation was leading. She had mentioned in one of their talks that she had seen a house in Santa Cruz that she liked.

'I'm sorry,' she said, 'I can't come with you.'

'You are stubborn,' he said.

On impulse she said, 'René, don't go.'

Confused, he shook his head, looking sad.

The drive from La Paz airport to the city has a sense of spiralling down and it matched Katya's mood. That night she went to the movies with her mother and aunt. The president called her soon after midnight, sounding depressed.

'I want to come back as quickly as possible,' he said.

When Katya awoke the following morning, she still felt troubled; she did not want to answer the phone. She recalls going to the hairdresser at 1 pm in a bad mood. When she returned home, she saw that her mother appeared distressed.

Katya knew instantly that her husband, René Barrientos, the president of Bolivia, was dead. 'Where?' she asked before her mother had a chance to say anything. 'How?'

Her mother, white-faced, did not answer.

'What happened to René?' Katya demanded.

'He's okay,' said her mother.

'No, he is not,' Katya said quietly.

Katya decided she would go immediately to Cochabamba. Some military friends came to the house and one offered to take her there. Her mother pleaded with her not to go. It was difficult for Katya to think clearly. If she went to Cochabamba, what was her status? Was she the widow of the president?

Would the government accept such a claim? Did she want to make this claim?

On the way to the airport, she heard a report on the car radio denying rumours that the president was dead, but passing the presidential palace she saw the flags at half-mast. She started crying and turned back home. Katya stayed in La Paz. And it was soon confirmed that he was dead. Her overwhelming feeling was of sadness.

The marriage had lasted just a month and was never consummated. They had never spent a day or night together as a married couple. She would later say: 'I started to love this man the day he died.'

President Barrientos's helicopter had hit power lines outside Cochabamba and burst into flames. The cause of the crash was in dispute. People in the vicinity reported hearing gunshots, but government sources said the gunshots were from ammunition exploding in the flames, and that the crash was caused by pilot error. The popular belief was clear-cut, however: it was an assassination.

Katya took little interest in the argument. René was dead. She cried frequently, ate very little and became ill. The president's body was laid out in the cathedral of La Paz for an official mourning period. She wanted to go the cathedral but felt she could not. A radio news program reported that the president's widow was at the cathedral carrying his ceremonial sword. When Katya heard this, she experienced a wave of melancholy, but it was not related to envy.

The brother-in-law of the president's official widow visited Katya asking for her silence and co-operation.

'Tell her not to worry,' Katya told him. 'It's okay. The president is dead. That is all.'

But Katya was wrong; there was more to come.

As the debate over the president's death switched from the cause of the crash to the motivation for an assassination, one prime suspect emerged: Tinino Rico Toro.

He was said to have two motives for assassinating Barrientos. One: he was the right-hand man of the former president, General Alfredo Ovando, who months after the crash staged a coup to regain the presidency and; two, he was the recently divorced husband of Katya Rivas.

In the end, nothing was found to link Tinino directly to the crash. He had an alibi. There was circumstantial evidence suggesting Tinino had been involved in the killing of another man who had witnessed the helicopter crash, but no charges were laid. While Tinino was expelled from the armed forces during this time, not even that stuck as shortly afterwards he was brought back in as President Ovando's right-hand man.

For Katya, therefore, it was not life after Che, but life after René that became the challenge. It was extremely difficult. She was the widow of the president and in death she loved him, but she could not attend his funeral. His name was now on her passport but amid the whirl of rumours, the most common belief was that she had just been one of his later mistresses. In the period of mourning, and even after, she stopped going to church; people stared at her.

She lost her job at the mining company because the Ovando government did not want her there. From being the First Lady of Bolivia, albeit secretly, she was now an unemployed single mother struggling to raise her two young children. And she carried the burden of a shady reputation.

In the wake of all of this, Katya left Bolivia and took her children to Lima in Peru where she found work at the Bolivian airline office. She stayed there for almost a year, before her father's ill health brought her back to La Paz.

Her father died and Katya suddenly had to be the main breadwinner. But unable to get a job, she was forced to find other ways to provide for her children and mother. She made lollies, grew plants in flowerpots and made textiles, such as table covers, by hand. She lived this more ordinary life for 18 years. There was no reason to suspect the spotlight would ever fix on her again.

'I had several men propose marriage,' explained Katya about those years. 'But I was afraid I would lose me if I married again. Then in 1987, I caught up with my old boss from Peru, Hugo. He had lived abroad most of that time as manager of the Bolivian airline in countries like Brazil, Chile and Panama. We saw each other for six months and then we agreed to get married. I was still afraid to get married and the only thing I remember is that when I signed the marriage certificate, I prayed: "My Lord, help me because this must be the final one." I had faith in God, but I did not walk His way. Hugo was an atheist and we married outside the Church.

'It was 9 September 1987. I was 43 years; he was 63.'

Hugo was a modest, conservative man. You could describe him as the antithesis of Tinino Rico Toro and René Barrientos. The marriage gave even more strength to the notion that Katya Rivas need never fear the glare of the public spotlight again.

Fifteen

What to Believe

I admit I was floored by the complexity of Katya's life story and the struggles she had faced and overcome. I did a number of follow-up interviews with different people who knew her at that time, all of which confirmed what she had told me, the most memorable of which was with her ex-husband, Tinino Rico Toro.

He was a reasonably handsome man of about 70, elegantly dressed and groomed, wearing a yellow cravat, like a '50s film star. He sat himself in an ornate antique chair.

'If you have come here to get me to say something bad about my former wife, you are wasting your time,' he opened, but in the very next sentence, without a question being asked, continued, 'You know she has a reputation.'

While I was still taking in those two sentences, he went on. 'But I have a reputation too, you know. I was a cavalry officer . . . in my uniform, handsome. I had the finest-looking horses, the smartest cars, and, on my arm, always the most beautiful woman: Miss Cochabamba; the runner-up in Miss Peru; all of them. I had the best.'

I was startled by the grossness of his ego, but I had at least established that Katya's claims of his philandering seemed well supported. He was difficult to interview, contradicting himself, ignoring questions and continuing to speak over the interpreter. On the question of being the main suspect in the assassination of President René Barrientos, however, I persisted.

He smiled and shrugged. 'How could I? And I can prove it was impossible. I was in a restaurant with a witness several hours away from where the helicopter crashed. It would have been impossible for me to get there, shoot him and get back in time. Impossible.'

I moved to alleged murder number two, that of a labour leader who claimed to have witnessed seeing Rico Toro at the helicopter crash site.

'So where were you when this man was murdered?' I asked.

'I was out of the country. I had been gone 15 days. I could not have done it.' He went into a longwinded speech on the jealousy of his military colleagues, mostly because they lacked his intellect. He voluntarily denied having tortured political prisoners when he was chief of intelligence, and then, as his pièce de résistance, he voluntarily denied a third murder allegation, saying he was again out of the country.

It was a fascinating interview. He could be at once charming and completely rude. After three hours, the translator was in tears and Ron was asleep. But for me it was worth the discomfort. If Katya had told me about his ego and his insensitivity, I would have been tempted to think I was listening to a disgruntled ex-wife. But her story, which had seemed so fantastical, was true.

It reminded me of an interview I was granted with President Ferdinand Marcos of the Philippines at a time of martial law in that country. Years earlier, Marcos had been convicted of the murder of a man who had defeated his father in a political election. The man had been shot from some distance through a bathroom window. Marcos was a champion marksman. Marcos was tried a second time in a court which his opponents asserted was politically contrived. This time he was acquitted, but like Rico Toro, his guilt or innocence was left to float in the court of public opinion.

'Mr President,' I'd asked, 'did you kill that man?'

He smiled and replied, 'The court said that I didn't.'

'Another court said you did,' I responded.

Again, he smiled, but made no reply.

It was an exchange I spent many hours trying to understand. Why would the president not deny that he was a murderer?

After some time, I realised what it was about: image. If people thought he was guilty, was that such a bad thing? Did it not make him a tough guy? Somebody to be reckoned with? Was it not a matter of honour to kill your father's enemy?

And so, with a narcissist like Rico Toro. Was it not a matter of honour to be seen to have killed the man who stole your wife? In the early '90s, some 14 years after Katya divorced him, Rico Toro was also extradited to the United States on cocaine trafficking charges. He spent two years in custody but was freed before it reached trial and without any evidence being offered. It all added to the image.

I had to admit that the total sum of my research made me think of Katya differently – she was far from an ordinary Bolivian woman. I couldn't quite connect her past with the woman I saw in front of me today: that she could have been a president's secret wife and widow, and years later be the person through whom God chose to send messages. It seemed unbelievable.

But I knew the first part of her story to be true: it had all checked out.

What I didn't know yet was whether, more than a quarter century after the events in her earlier life, this changed woman with a very different story to tell was to be believed again.

It was reassuring to find that I was not the only doubter. When I asked Katya's brother Richie how he had reacted to claims that God had spoken to his sister he smiled, then pointed to his smile.

'That's how I reacted,' he said. 'At first, she didn't make claims about herself, but she started going to prayer groups and talking about the Virgin Mary, and God, and the Church; each time with more insistence. It got to the point where when my wife suggested we go visit my mother at Katya's house, I would say no, because she would only talk about the Virgin and the Church. Her husband, Hugo, was an atheist and there were many arguments. The atmosphere was heavy.'

But they did visit again, and Richie explained that on that day, he smelt a fragrance at the house, a very pleasant one. He thought it was a spray.

Richie paused before going on.

'But one day we went to see Katya and she said the Virgin had told her something. I said: "Where?" She said: "Here." I shut up and told my wife this woman is crazy and we went home and I was really worried. I thought Katya was really getting crazy. People started making jokes about going to Katya's house to hear what the Virgin has had to say.

'One night my wife, Ana, came home from seeing Katya and said: "I have been thinking that Jesus was persecuted and maybe we are doing the same thing to Katya. Perhaps we should show more interest in her." So we asked Katya if she could show us any message and she read a message from Jesus.

'As she read it, I understood that it was impossible for her to be the author of such extraordinary texts.'

The Archbishop of Cochabamba, René Fernandez, also had doubts and when I spoke with him, he was direct. 'Many knew Catalina's [Katya's] life and would say how could God, Jesus, present himself to a sinner?'

'What was your reaction?' I asked.

'The same as everyone,' he said. 'Doubts.'

'When you are told things that are extraordinary, you are inclined to believe they are not true. Even when I was called to her house to be present in the moment she was with the stigmata. Her husband took a small piece of cotton and wiped the blood on her foot. But I left with a lot of doubts because anybody can cut themselves or do something that will start bleeding.

'When I came back the next day, however, I examined her hands and feet and they had absolutely nothing, not even a scar.

'But I was still careful. I did not want to make this too public.'

I asked him what his colleagues in the Church thought.

'I know that many, a greater part, my brothers, bishops, outright refuse to accept any revelations that Katya might have,' he said.

'Is this then a brave step by you to give the Imprimatur to these writings of Katya?' I asked. The Catholic Church's Imprimatur can only be given by the relevant bishop. It means the writing is not against Church teaching and is worthy of belief.

He considered the question.

'For me to approve, or put a prologue to, her books, I have firstly read them many times over and found there is no theological mistake. Even if they are not revelations, they do merit to be studied; they are a confirmation of the gospels.'

The Archbishop then added what Ron had been so insistent about: 'Katya has not had the preparation [education] in literature or theology to write these messages.'

By now, I was happy to accept the consensus: Katya Rivas was not the author of these well-written spiritual messages. So who was?

For Katya's believers, the answer was easy. It was mostly Jesus or occasionally the Virgin Mary or some other heavenly figure. But the non-believers were in the majority in their belief that this was a huge deceit. They, however, were not concerned about the source.

I was.

What if there were some Svengali-like figure behind all this? If such a person were to emerge *after* my report went to air, I would not need critics to point out my failure. I would know.

My first suspect – well, my only suspect – was the intellectual Doctor Ricardo Castanon. But the more I learnt about his relationship with Katya Rivas, the more I saw serious points of conflict. Their relationship got off to a poor start when the Church in Cochabamba invited Ricardo to make a psychological evaluation of Katya in 1995.

'Katya was then 52 years of age,' Ricardo told me. 'She said she was having inner locutions [hearing voices]. She was not always so close to the Catholic Church but she had experienced a deep conversion. I studied her but I could not find any technical proof, any technical reference that she was telling the truth. I didn't say she was lying, I just couldn't say something extraordinary is happening. I told her that perhaps she was having normal and holy inspirations.'

That hurt Katya.

When I asked her about Ricardo's early opinion, she grimaced. 'Yes, he said I should not call them messages. Just inspirations.'

'How did you react?' I asked.

'I knew they were messages from Jesus, but I agreed to call the first books *Inspirations*. He said that if God wanted me to make this public, He would give a proof.'

'What did you think of Ricardo at that time?'

Katya did not answer but shrugged and made a whimsical face.

The 'proof' that Ricardo sought came, in his view, about two years later when he visited Katya in hospital and saw that she was experiencing wounds consistent with the stigmata, the wounds of Christ.

In the meantime, however, there was another discordance between the two.

In early October 1996, Katya had talked about a message she said she received from Jesus which made reference to the Feast of the Rosary. But the date in the message put the feast on 8 October. The calendar of feast days of the Catholic Church, however, dates the Feast of the Rosary as 7 October.

Katya learned that Ricardo had raised this discrepancy at a meeting in Miami.

'If Jesus dictates to her, there should be no errors,' he said.

Again, Katya was hurt.

In her book *The Door to Heaven*, Katya reports this message from the Lord:

IT DOES NOT PLEASE ME FOR YOU TO QUESTION MY MESSAGES.

You continue to worry that 8 October was not the Feast of

> *the Rosary. Good, even though it does not please Me that you question My messages. I will explain it to you so you may calm My son NN [standing for 'not named' but referring to Ricardo Castanon]. I know the fragility of faith in human nature. On 8 October in the year 1483 a devotion towards an incomplete version of the Hail Mary was started in many countries. It was not Dominic de Guzman who invented the Rosary; the first part of the Hail Mary had been prayed in the year 1150. Instead of praying the 150 psalms, 150 Hail Mary's were prayed.*
>
> *Later, Pius V through a letter and an encyclical, recommended the praying of the Rosary as is done today. Then in 1878, Leon XIII asked that the Feast of the Virgin of the Rosary be celebrated on 7 October and he dedicated 12 encyclicals and 23 documents (one later being annulled) to the prayer of the Rosary.*
>
> *Are you more at ease now My daughter? That is the history. If they still have questions, consult with the theologians.*

Ron Tesoriero had told me this story before I came to Bolivia to impress on me the virtues of Katya's writings, but he had not told me that the man who questioned the 'mistake' was Ricardo Castanon.

'It is the only allegation of a mistake in her writings that I have heard of,' Ron had said. 'And just look at the answer.'

At the time I had questioned how easily the information in Katya's response could be assessed. Ron explained he had undertaken the exercise himself and taken a significant amount of material from the *Catholic Encyclopedia* through the internet. It confirmed that there was evidence that the Rosary may have begun before St Dominic (against accepted Catholic belief). But most important for Ron's argument was that Katya's message contained additional and more concise information, including the seemingly forgotten encyclical of Pius V.

I became far more interested in this instance of Katya's writings being challenged once I knew Ricardo was involved, as I was actually more intent on examining the relationship between Katya and Ricardo than the writings themselves.

But this story seemed to suggest it was unlikely that Ricardo was the puppetmaster I had been hunting for.

Where did all this leave me? Theologically confused and without a suspect. I decided to revert to my usual reporting practices: film what you can, as best you can; question as best you can and edit the results fairly. Leave judgment to the viewers.

Wow, why hadn't I thought of that before?

I went back to the old monastery alone, ordered a beer and headed for the charming old rotunda; it had become my friend. It occurred to me that any time I needed thinking space it was there just for me, and I reached for another old friend, a small cigar. The *cerveza* was cold, the day was pleasantly warm, and the cigar was comforting. The occasional '*Buenos dias*' from passing employees made me feel at home.

Now I was ready. I pulled out my notebook and started to write and it seemed that each thought I put on paper eased the clutter in my mind:

1. Get out of your own head. Stop being judge and jury; if you can't film it, forget it. Evidence yes; judgment no.
2. Stop worrying about the messages. Film Katya writing, get some brief critiques and then let go! A deep discussion on the theological or literary merits will kill this program.
3. Drop the paranoia on Castanon: he makes sense and I can find no indication of deceit.
4. Enjoy Katya's company. This whole film revolves around

her having the stigmata before our cameras. She WILL or she WON'T. Anxiety is useless.
5. Katya is not the only alleged mystic in the world. Who else? Where else? What else?
6. If the strangeness of these supernatural stories proves true or false – IT IS NOT MY PROBLEM. I am only a reporter; I can only do my best.
7. Most important, order another *cerveza*!

Boy, that felt good. Now I was ready to start shooting.

Part Five

Signs from God

Sixteen

Following the Trail

After my moment of clarity in the rotunda, I knew exactly what I needed to do next.

All of Katya's stigmata had occurred on Fridays in the past, and so, with Easter about three weeks away, we guessed that there was a strong chance her next one would take place then. We needed this to happen for us to have a show. We were willing it to happen. I definitely had Good Friday on my mind, as we nervously awaited the big day.

I decided to use the few weeks we had in the meantime to seek out and investigate other miraculous happenings – with the hope we could get something to happen on camera.

So I was now on the road with a camera crew, tracking down any lead that sounded credible. Katya had told me of a woman in Mexico City who she believed to be an authentic mystic. Among other things, this woman had built an orphanage about two hours outside Mexico City, and that's where we had found her.

Her name was Ernestina. She was an older woman, calm and dignified, and there was no doubting her commitment to

God. Her work included the establishment of two religious orders, one for priests and one for nuns. As far as I could tell, she had provided much of the necessary finance. Two of her sons were priests. Ernestina sought no publicity and did not volunteer any mystical experiences, but she agreed to answer my questions.

The day of our meeting, she came towards me smiling, holding two babies in her arms, each a few months old.

The camera was rolling.

'Each of these little ones was thrown away soon after birth,' she told me. 'We are very blessed to have them with us.'

She passed the first one to me.

'This little boy was tossed into a pile of trash, but somebody heard him crying and dug him out. Fortunately, they brought him to us; he was very weak but look at him now.'

She looked down at the baby she still held.

'This one is a girl and it is even more amazing that she survived. A man noticed a feral dog circling something in the middle of a field. He felt something was wrong, so he walked into the field and found this newborn baby. When he brought her here, he told me he believed the dog was about to eat the baby.'

I could think of nothing useful to say or ask.

As I looked down at these two little wonders, the hand of one caught the hand of the other and it stayed that way. They were holding hands. It was a special moment and it tested my emotions, but it had not taken us one step closer to measuring or testing any mystical relationship between God and man.

I had been told that in Ernestina's chapel was a consecrated host, a wafer of bread known as the Eucharist, in which many could see the face of the crucified Christ. My first request was to see and film this piece of bread.

'Yes, you may,' she said quietly, 'but I must warn you that many see nothing.'

I took her warning as an indication that this could be authentic. It seemed to me that if an image had been fraudulently embedded into the host, then everybody would see it. One of her sons opened the tabernacle and removed an ornate frame known as a monstrance. The host was in the centre behind glass. I looked but saw nothing. The members of the camera crew looked, but also saw nothing. Our cameraman, Greg Barbera, put his 'close-up' lens right up to the glass and looked at the host through the camera. He saw nothing. There were several visitors present and I recall two saying they saw the image of Christ very clearly; they were excited and emotional.

I was not.

'Ernestina, do you always see this image clearly?'

'Yes,' she replied simply.

She seemed such a decent woman and she was asking for nothing, not even my belief. There was nothing to argue; nothing to film. Her son was putting the monstrance back into the tabernacle, his expression and his movements devoid of judgment. I decided to give it one last shot.

'Ernestina, do you have anything of a mystical nature which we can film?'

She understood my predicament and smiled.

'Well, I'm not sure if you think it is a proof, but I will tell you and you can decide . . . Some years ago, Jesus told me to buy the house next door and dig a well for water. I protested because Mexico City is built on a swamp and even our cathedral is falling down. To get water you can drink, you must drill at some depth and you may still not get the water.'

'What did you do?' I asked.

'Well, of course I did what Jesus asked me. I bought the house and asked the men to dig a well. They had to dig only about eight feet and found clean water. Do you want to see it?'

We went with Ernestina to see the well. It was shallow and perfectly clean, and I drank from it; the taste was pure and there was neither moss nor stain on the walls.

'What is the purpose of this well?' I asked.

'I don't know,' she said, 'perhaps Jesus was testing my obedience because I did not believe you could build such a well in this city. But now people come and drink and pray and many claim they have been healed.'

'You have miracles?'

'I don't know. We don't make any claims, but people come back with little notes of thanks to God.'

'Do you ever talk to their doctors?' I asked.

'No, it is between the people who pray, and God.'

Although there was definitely something unusual about this well's fresh water, there wasn't really much for us to prove or disprove about it on camera or through speaking with Ernestina.

Was it really only a week before that I had found such comfort in the rotunda: no more useless anxiety, just do what you always do: film what you can and leave judgment to the viewers. Simple.

Now in addition to fragrances I couldn't film and fresh human blood that I couldn't test, I had visions that only other people could see and healings without names or medical evidence. Not to mention fresh water from a dirty swamp. How much geological evidence would I need to prove that was or was not a gift from God?

If investigation truly is 90 per cent perspiration and 10 per cent inspiration, well, I was perspiring. Heavily. My desperation to film Katya experiencing the stigmata was growing exponentially. We had nothing else.

After Mexico City, our next stop found us lost in the back streets of Monterrey, Mexico, where the streets and alleys were laid out in a most confusing way. We were looking for the house of a woman named Mila, another mystic who Katya believed to be authentic. It wasn't easy – there were streets without names and houses without numbers – but the locals knew Mila and told us where to go. The crew started unloading their equipment, while I went in to meet my newest mystic.

Mila's home was seriously humble: a tiny bedroom at the back and the front room which had effectively been given over to the neighbours as a chapel. There were three apartments in the building, and they shared a common laundry and kitchen. It was so poorly constructed that the concrete stairs to the upper apartment actually failed to connect to the building.

Mila was very shy and spoke no English. She opened her hands and looked in the direction of an altar in the corner as if to say: 'This is why you are here.'

There was a very well-known image of the Sacred Heart of Jesus, heavily stained as if it may have bled in previous times. There was an image of the Virgin Mary among other icons, and there were many roses and hundreds of rose petals.

Mila suddenly picked up a picture of the Virgin, an image known as Our Lady Help of Christians, and handed it to me. She pointed to the right eye.

There was a tear forming.

I turned to the cameraman, 'Quick, Greg! Camera.'

As he hurriedly prepped his camera, I looked carefully at the image. It was covered by glass on both sides and bound by a wooden frame. The tear was real. Greg filmed it and it soon evaporated and disappeared. It was a small tear, but it was 'our' tear.

It *happened*! And we had it on tape!

What did it mean? I had no time for such considerations. Holding the image as Greg filmed, I ad-libbed to the camera: 'The important thing with this image is that it is sandwiched between two pieces of glass. When you turn it around, you see it is transparent from the back and quite clearly, with this simple print, there is no room in there for any device which could fabricate weeping.'

More than two decades later, I can find no reason to change one word of that spontaneous reaction.

The front room of Mila's home really functioned as a chapel where neighbours would come to pray. This was due to an image that appeared on the floor of that room – an image that resembled the most famous icon of the Virgin in Latin America, Our Lady of Guadalupe. Mila explained to us that the image grew stronger and sharper every time she mopped the uneven concrete floor. It was a mysterious image: not painted, not dyed and not, to our eyes, on the surface of the concrete. In terms of scientific testing, however, it was a little like Ernestina's well: how could we dig up her floor?

But it was at Mila's altar that we saw the most mysterious phenomena. When Mila's neighbours came to pray at the little altar in her front room, they would often bring roses. The petals tended to collect on the altar. In time, some of the petals seemed to reveal intricate religious images on them. Mila said the images appeared after she and her followers placed the petals in the pages of their prayer books. Sometimes it took a few hours for an image to appear. Others might appear over weeks.

'At first, we had these petals inside a book, and it had nothing on it. Then we prayed the rosary and this image appeared on it.'

These weren't vague shapes that people see in a piece of toast or a carrot and declare to be a vision of the Virgin. They were tiny, intricate images that clearly resembled known portraits of Jesus or His mother. One was clearly Our Lady of Guadalupe. Of course, like all such images, it raises the question that if these really were divinely created, would their creator have chosen to copy an artist's impression painted by someone who had no idea what the Virgin really looked like? Or would this divine creator choose to copy a well-known icon simply as a sign that people would understand?

The rose petals presented a chance to conduct scientific tests. I asked Mila if we could submit the petals with the images to testing by botanists, scientists or experts in art fraud. She readily agreed.

The tear was indeed another mystery, but we had seen it happen and, most importantly, we had filmed it. The liquid in the tear had evaporated and we could see no sign of any residue. There can be a salt precipitation from tears, but we could see nothing to scrape for a laboratory sample. It seemed to me that this particular mystery did not call for an attempt at scientific testing. The images on the rose petals, however, offered great promise and I thought we could learn a lot through a relatively simple analysis.

When saying goodbye to Mila, I was impressed again by her calmness; she was not excited by the television cameras, she was not excited by the prospect of her little 'miracles' being exposed to the world. And if she was fraudulently manufacturing the images on the petals, then she certainly showed no concern at the prospect of being exposed by the experts.

'Do you care what the tests will tell us?' I asked her.

'It would be of interest to me,' she replied, 'and it would be proof that all that is happening here is true.'

'Do you know why it happens?'

'It is a reward,' she said, 'a reward for faith and prayer.'

For me, it was a small reward for persistence. There had been more than a few occasions when I had questioned myself about the validity of making this television program. Now, in one day, we had both a tear forming on an image and images formed on rose petals. I would have no hesitation in broadcasting that tear forming and posing the question: 'Is this a Sign from God?' As for the outcome of any testing of the petals, well, that was not my problem. The images existed, they were unique and they were puzzling and it seemed to me that any analysis, whether scientific or artistic, would be easy for viewers to follow.

As we bumped our way out of the back streets of Monterrey, I felt satisfied. It had been a good day's work.

Next, we turned to Doctor Ricardo Castanon. Ricardo claimed that he had registered specific and dramatic changes in brainwave activity at the moment that a person had said that he or she was in the presence of Jesus. I asked him to explain.

'Well, firstly, as an atheist, I believed it would not be difficult to prove that many of these supernatural claims were false. If not fraudulently, then perhaps through some abnormality of the brain. About six years ago, I was examining a woman in the United States, a woman who said she had visions of the Virgin Mary and Jesus. It was about the time I started working with Ron Tesoriero.

'Ron asked me to explain how I could do this, just as you are asking now. I told him that I was astonished that a woman could make such claims, have thousands of people believe her, and yet nobody makes any tests. Here in the United States you can study anything, I told him. They have studied from which side of a bicycle a child is more likely to fall. But where are the scientists when these claims are made?'

'How did you do it?' I asked.

'Well, I am sure you know what the term EEG means. It is an electroencephalogram. It is not new, but it does an excellent job in monitoring activity in the brain. It can discover things like epilepsy or tumours and show you where the problem is; it establishes if brain activity is normal. But for our purposes, presuming there are no abnormalities, it establishes patterns of wavelengths, and it is not at all complex.

'There are four types of brainwaves and the bottom, or slowest, is called Delta. A person reaches the Delta state in a coma or a very deep sleep. You cannot communicate with a person in that state.'

Ricardo had already run this test on a number of people who had claimed to be receiving interventions from God, and he had got some interesting results. At the time when his subjects were reciting their received 'messages' to others in the room, their brainwaves indicated they were in Delta state – and should have been in a deep sleep. Ricardo had not, however, run the test on Katya.

That was interesting. It gave us our next test.

Seventeen

Testing Faith

Back in Mexico City, I hailed one of the city's unique two-door Volkswagen taxis to get back to our high-rise hotel and climbed into the doorless back seat. It felt a little claustrophobic; if the cab was involved in a crash there was no easy way out. Our hotel was situated on a roundabout where about six streets converged and vehicles competed more with willpower than with rules to get through the intersection. While we sat there, two cars collided and I watched as the drivers put up their dukes and started throwing punches, gridlocking a few thousand cars in the process.

It suddenly occurred to me that I was severely distracted. I knew something was wrong, but I didn't know what.

Ricardo Castanon had claimed success with a relatively simple but purely scientific test: hook a patient up to an EEG and, barring any abnormalities of the brain, if the patient registers brainwaves in the Delta state and communicates at the same time, then the science of neurology can't explain that. In our case, if that patient happens to say she is talking to Jesus, then the claim of such an apparently bizarre supernatural phenomenon is then matched by an equally strong scientific question.

Katya had agreed to undergo testing without reservation or even conversation, and the day of the test had finally come. Ricardo's confidence was calm and strong: it was clear to me that he was steadily emerging from his chrysalis of atheism. I should have been feeling more enthusiastic myself. This was exactly the type of scientific test I needed. What was my problem?

The answer slowly dawned.

It was Ricardo.

Specifically, Ricardo's test. It was a unique examination which he had devised, and which I had allowed him to organise in full, right down to finding the neurologist. It was not a question of distrusting Ricardo per se, but a scientific experiment must be seen to have no possibility of contamination. That's what was worrying me. I wondered what I could do about it at this late stage.

I had no sooner returned to my room when Ricardo arrived, looking troubled.

'I'm afraid we have a problem,' he said. 'The neurologist has cancelled. He won't do it.'

'Why not?' I asked.

'He gives no answer. I think it is because I declined to tell him the purpose of the test . . . what we are looking for.'

'Ricardo, can we get another neurologist?'

'I didn't tell you how difficult it was to get this one. It won't be easy. For today or even tomorrow it may not be possible.'

I called Katya, Father Renzo and Ron Tesoriero, who all joined us in my hotel room. Katya brought with her a friend who was a local. This friend had a friend who worked for a doctor who knew people. After a frenzy of phone calls, we had a new neurologist. It was one of the few occasions I had seen Ricardo show stress and he was clearly relieved. I was more so.

If the experiment failed, it would not actually prove that Katya was *not* authentic. If it was successful, however, it would add a significant argument to support her case, in that she would be disproving an accepted scientific idea that it was impossible to communicate while experiencing Delta-state brainwaves. Even this, though, would not stand alone as proof that she was receiving messages from God.

But for me the testing was a good and necessary step to take on the path of investigating Katya's claims. If Katya's experiences were true, I was prepared to build the case brick by brick. In many ways, there was more pressure on Ricardo than on Katya. It was his experiment and he believed in it.

I decided I still needed to know more about Ricardo Castanon.

Ricardo Castanon had finished high school as the top student in his school in La Paz, however, he was not necessarily happy with the honour. As a youth, and even more today, he felt strongly that the education system was weighted too heavily towards grades, honours and diplomas, and away from a genuine search for greater knowledge in a creative manner.

When I first asked Ricardo if I could interview him, he hesitated, and after some thought replied, 'I will write something for you.'

I was extremely disappointed and thought he was being evasive. Rarely has my judgment been so wrong.

He returned with a 13-page mini-biography which allowed me into his mind and his heart. His story went something like this.

'When I was 10 years old, I went to school in the mornings. But I felt that I was not learning sufficiently, therefore my father registered me in another school in the afternoons. When the morning school became aware of this, they informed me that I could not attend both schools. Thus, I decided to abandon the morning school because they had misunderstood my intentions.

'In 1967, I registered at the Faculty of Medicine in the State University. I was interested in psychology, but in Bolivia this career did not yet exist.

'The universities in Europe put me in contact with professors who cited their own texts, in which I found recompilation of other authors and very rarely were they the ones who wrote about their original thoughts or investigations.

'I found myself in Rome, a young university student dedicated to psychology, looking for a clinical specialty. Psychology in Italy focused on the brain and speech a lot. But I asked myself, for example, what else did a word produce in the brain, aside from thoughts and ideas? I was interested in knowing what chemical changes occurred in neurons . . .

'Psychology interested me, but so did philosophy and literature. A Spanish professor introduced me to existentialism where I encountered the writings of Jean-Paul Sartre, which would change my life.

'To live in Rome at a youthful age is a privilege. I was the favourite son of Artemis, Romulus and Remus and Caesar; brother to many gladiators, admirer of Michelangelo and relative to all those who had forged the culture that I drank without satiation . . .

'The time between the years of 1969 and 1972 are the most interesting because they cover the years of the birth of the University Revolution in France. Hair was worn long, songs of protest reigned and the majority of my companions admired Che Guevara, even though they did not know a lot about him. That didn't stop them from putting pictures of him smoking a pipe up on their walls. Life was lived with an air of independence, of anarchy. Even in Holy Rome, there were priests who said to my companions that if they loved their girlfriends and they had prenuptial relations, it was not a sin.

'I listened with respect, but I already knew that my Christian spirit was slowly fading, with my Sartrean readings. I went to the famous Maudsley Hospital in London to listen to Professor Hans Eysenck where I found the greatest wealth dedicated to the study of depression, which then served me in my work for my doctorate. He was the teacher who truly inspired much of what I would do later. He sensed also that psychology had to do with biology and genetics.

'Having graduated and become a director of a psychosomatic clinic in Germany, I then took a literature course at a university in northern Italy. I travelled to Italy every 15 days, something I did with much enthusiasm. Until a professor of literature thwarted my parallel career by asking in an exam the names of the characters in the works of Cesare Pavese. I knew the principal characters, but he wanted all the names. I also was a university professor. Never would I have behaved in such a manner with my students. This was not for the love of knowledge of literature. Rising, I told him that such an academic exam was disrespectful and that if he wanted names, he should read the telephone directory.'

After reading his mini-biography, I now saw Ricardo Castanon through different eyes. From his pages I saw his secret. Hidden beneath his cloak of pure academia, Ricardo was a Renaissance man: a lover with the soul of a poet.

★

Signs from God

Back in the neurological department of the Angeles Hospital of Mexico City, an eminent teaching hospital, I was talking with the chief neurologist, Doctor Víctor Pelle. We had made the appointment only that morning and his eyes were sparkling almost mischievously. This was a very unusual situation for him; no referring medical practitioner, no psychiatrist, and he had been told of no symptoms. His eyes showed his curiosity – fortunately with good humour.

An EEG suite is not unlike a television studio. The neurologist is like the director sitting at a desk full of nobs and dials, in an enclosed booth overlooking the room where the action is to take place: in the case of an EEG test, this booth overlooks the room where the patient is. It is very important for this story to note that the glass which separates the neurologist's booth, with its facility for the EEG printout, is completely soundproof from the room below.

A technician attached electrodes to Katya's skull to transmit signals from various parts of her brain to Doctor Pelle's machine. Ron and I were squeezed into Doctor Pelle's little booth where we were to record the reactions of Doctor Pelle and film any relevant parts of the EEG printout. Ricardo Castanon and Father Renzo Sessolo were in the room below with Katya who was prepped by the technician, with little bits of tape now holding the electrodes in place on her scalp. Our cameraman, Greg Barbara, was also in that room with them, filming. I walked the few steps down to the lower room and approached Katya.

'Katya, has it occurred to you that if you don't get the results we are looking for, you might be letting people down?' I asked.

'No,' she said. 'I know the Lord is with me and He will do whatever is necessary.'

'So that makes you confident?'

'Yes . . . always,' she replied.

There could not be the slightest doubt. This woman was completely and utterly relaxed. Similarly, while you would never really say that he was relaxed because of his usual intensity, Ricardo certainly showed no signs of nerves or doubt either. He knew very well that this was a trial for him also, maybe an even greater trial because he was the one who claimed success in this unique neurological experiment.

There was one other interesting aspect of the test. The Delta state, that state only seen in deep sleep or coma, registers on the EEG somewhere between zero and four hertz. In all of Ricardo's previous tests, he had told us that the specific reading recorded had been exactly three hertz and they had occurred in exactly the same sequence and lasting only as long as the patient said they were communicating with God. All of this, of course, defies scientific explanation.

Ron had actually been through this process before, when he and Ricardo tested the American mystic Nancy Fowler. As I said earlier, from my observations of her running around that paddock with her followers, I found her unconvincing. But to give her credit, she never claimed to have seen anything on that day and even admitted that she may have 'lost her grace'. When they had tested her with an EEG three years earlier, she had gone into a Delta state during the period where she claimed to be communicating with Jesus. To their knowledge, that was the first time such a test had been done on someone claiming to communicate with the Lord.

Before Katya's test started – and with Ron's camera rolling – I asked Doctor Pelle if he knew why he was testing this patient.

'No,' he said.

Signs from God

I asked him to explain the different states of the mind and he explained each of the four: I did not indicate in any way which of those four states we were looking for.

However, I did say, 'So in the Delta state, it is impossible for the patient to communicate?'

'That is correct,' he said. 'There can be exceptions when there are abnormalities like, for example a tumour or epilepsy.'

The experiment began and for the first thirty minutes Katya underwent routine baseline tests to check that her brain was healthy. During the early stages, she registered regular Alpha and Beta brainwave patterns indicating no abnormalities.

With Greg Barbara filming in the patient's room, Ricardo then said to Katya, 'Now begin to pray.'

As Katya started praying, her brainwave pattern slowed significantly, but only on the left-hand side of the brain.

Back in the booth, Doctor Pelle began to speculate on the possible cause of this change.

'This is abnormal. From a neurological point of view, it could be epilepsy, if there is no tumour.'

'Is what we are seeing abnormal?' I ask.

'Yes,' he said. 'On the left-hand side.'

Katya continued to pray, and her breathing seemed to become heavier. Then the next part of the test, where she was exposed to the stimuli of light, began. Katya's abnormal pattern remained.

'The light is to get faster now,' explained Doctor Pelle, speaking to Ron's camera up in the booth.

Ricardo placed a crucifix in Katya's hands, and instructed her. 'Begin to talk to Him as you do always. If Jesus begins to talk to you, let us know.'

Father Renzo then placed a picture of Jesus in Katya's hands.

After a short moment, Katya indicated that she was seeing Jesus in the room, whispering, 'Our Lord is present.'

'How do you see Him?' asked Ricardo.

'He is standing here.'

As Katya then took Eucharist from Father Renzo, I could see in the EEG that her brainwaves were slowing into the Delta state. We could also see down into the room that Katya had begun speaking.

'This is very abnormal,' Doctor Pelle said, pointing at the screen.

'He's only looking at me,' Katya said, lying down with her eyes closed, before proceeding to describe her vision to Ricardo.

Doctor Pelle explained that he had never seen such a thing before.

'From a neurological point of view, it could be epilepsy,' he said again.

What follows is an account pieced together from Ron's video in the booth, combined with the translated video of Katya in her room.

Shortly after Doctor Pelle had suggested epilepsy as a cause of what he was seeing, Katya said she has received a message from Christ. 'I have nothing wrong. Nothing wrong,' she said in Spanish.

Ricardo asked her what she meant. It didn't make sense to him, because they were in a room sealed off from Doctor Pelle, so neither he nor Katya could have heard the neurologist saying that it could be epilepsy.

'I know it,' she said. 'I know this.'

She seemed to be talking directly to the neurologist, apparently on instruction from Jesus.

'You think I am epileptic?' Katya said.

'Well, because of that malformation, I would think so,' Doctor Pelle answered in his sealed booth, speaking to me in English.

I didn't know what he was talking about because we couldn't hear Katya from where we were.

'He should know I am not epileptic,' she responded.

I'd later see it on film, but as it was unfolding, it was not making any sense to me. But I could see Katya's lips moving, and it slowly began to dawn on me.

They're having a conversation.

I felt the hairs on the back of my neck stand up. It was the first time in my life that I couldn't even find a question to ask.

When discussing the events of the test later, Doctor Pelle would say he was astounded.

'When she answered me, I felt something strange in my body . . . I think I had an out-of-body experience and I cannot explain it. I felt something in myself. I don't know.'

Doctor Pelle was clearly confused, not just by the response, but by the fact that he realised he'd stepped over this professional line and talked to a patient who he knew couldn't hear him.

Ron, too, reported that he had been aware that something was going on, but he didn't know what. He was more focused on ensuring he captured everything. It was only when we sat down to watch the raw tape that we really began to piece together what we'd just seen.

Interestingly, Katya told me afterwards that when she was praying and Father Renzo gave her Eucharist, she saw Jesus approach. She said He touched her on the left side of the head, which is important. That was where the abnormality first appeared in the EEG.

MIKE WILLESEE

I was intrigued and excited by the way the test had played out: at the very least, we had the bones of a good story. Whether it was more than that – just a 'story' – well, I could only hope time would reveal all, as at this stage, I had no idea what to believe.

Eighteen

Bearing Witness

We had made excellent progress, but we needed more. I'd promised Fox a stigmata. I don't know why – no-one had ever filmed one before to my knowledge. And the best I'd been able to get from Katya was that *if* she experienced a stigmata, we could film it. I had the notion that it would happen on Good Friday so I wanted to be ready.

As Easter approached, we flew back to Bolivia to get ready for the big day. We set ourselves up in Katya's home and started with another interview. I asked what it was like to experience a stigmata and when she was expecting it, but she suddenly broke off the conversation and paused, as if her mind was elsewhere.

She'd done this before and when she returned to the conversation, she'd say something like, 'Jesus has just said to me . . .'

The messages were never wild prophecies – they were usually just sensible advice. She didn't seem to be trying to draw attention to herself by saying such things.

On the first occasion that I had witnessed Jesus apparently speaking to Katya, it had really thrown me. *Is this for real? Do I believe this?* For some reason, despite the fact there were four of us there, I felt like I wasn't part of the group. I felt there was one group talking with Katya but that I was the audience, sitting back watching, which, physically, wasn't true. We were in a circle, but somehow I wasn't part of it.

That time, Jesus said we could ask Him questions, and the first opportunity went to Ron. Back then, I was totally hung up on the question of how I was going to make a program without any evidence. We had nothing. I couldn't wait for Ron to ask Jesus about this. But Ron started asking about something else and I got annoyed.

Ron, you've got an opportunity here. If He really is there, ask Him about the program! That's why we're here.

The others present also got their chance to ask Jesus questions through Katya. I was sitting back thinking, *Why don't they talk about my program?*

Like I wasn't part of it.

And then, Katya said Jesus was ready for my question. It shook me. I wasn't part of this process. I was an observer. I was forced to think of a question. In the end, I didn't quite ask a question – instead, I said, 'Well, Jesus, I'm worried about this program.'

Katya responded, 'You have many talents, Mike. I have given you talents, and you have used them sometimes well, and I am with you holding you by the hand.'

That shook me even more. *Is this Jesus talking to me? Is He really there?* It threw me. I didn't know how to handle this situation. It isn't something you get a lot of practice at. The strongest memory I have of that incident is that He basically said that I had nothing to worry about because He was holding me by the hand.

This time, as we did the pre-stigmata interview, when Katya turned back to me, she said, 'Jesus has just spoken to me. He said you've got it wrong. That maybe this is not the moment or time to take the samples you are looking for. Learn to trust in me more. This is not the right time.'

She said the stigmata would happen in Jesus' time, not ours. But that our patience would be rewarded.

I was frustrated. I'd been knocked back plenty of times before, but never by Jesus! We had to make the best of the situation, however, so we returned to Katya's the next day to interview her some more.

As we set up the lights and cameras in her lounge room again, she interrupted to say she'd received a new message from Jesus. She'd written it down in an ox blood-coloured book which she kept for all such conversations. She picked it up and read it for the cameras.

'In reference to Mike, he will see more marvellous things through me.'

I was scribbling it all down in my reporter's notebook, as Katya went on to say that not only would there be a full stigmata, but that Jesus had told her the date.

'The day after the day of Corpus Christi.'

Being brought up a Catholic, I knew the feast of Corpus Christi was the feast of Christ's body. It was a full nine weeks away. I was very disappointed. I was thinking as a television producer. It had cost us a lot of money to be there and we needed vision *now*.

'That gives us a lot to think about,' I said to Katya.

'And me also,' she answered, raising her eyebrows and giving a little laugh.

There was nothing for it but to wait. We all went home. It gave me time to freshen up on my theology. The feast of Corpus Christi is a public holiday in a lot of the Catholic world, including Bolivia. It's a 'moveable feast', set down for the first

Thursday after Trinity Sunday, which itself is eight weeks after Easter Sunday. It celebrates the real presence of Jesus' flesh and blood in the bread and wine of the Eucharist. It looked like Jesus had picked a date that was saying He was giving us His flesh and blood.

And He'd given us film rights.

And a schedule.

We had an appointment with God: 4 June 1999.

A week before the appointed day, I met Ron at Sydney airport to fly back to Cochabamba. I didn't understand at the time that I was taking my first sneaky steps back towards the faith of my childhood. But I was still excited. I believed that no stigmata had ever been filmed in its entirety. I had absolutely no guarantee that we would get to witness such a thing, but my focus was entirely on the fact that it would happen and that we would film it. You could say that I was obsessed with getting that footage.

Ron and I had travelled extensively together – we'd been overseas three times in the previous three months. So when I saw him at the airport, I didn't pay any attention to how he was looking. Even when he asked me to place his bag on the scales for him at the check-in counter, I didn't take much notice. And if he was giving off signals that he wasn't feeling so well on the flight, I didn't pick up on them. He certainly didn't complain. But on the long walk between terminals in Los Angeles to our connecting flight for Bolivia, I started to become a little alarmed when he could not keep up with me. I dropped my pace for him, but the slower I went, the slower he seemed to go. Something was wrong. I took his hand luggage. He made not the slightest protest.

Signs from God

When we got to Cochabamba, I again had to assist him, and when we got to the old monastery hotel, it just seemed automatic that I would carry the bags. Ron was given a room upstairs, only one flight, and without even looking at me he started limping up the stairs, leaving me with his bag.

Ron later told me that he was having a difficult internal argument with himself when he got on the plane in Sydney. His doctor had advised him not to take the trip and given him some pills if things got worse. By the time we got to Los Angeles, he was feeling so bad he'd begun to worry about not having updated his will and giving sufficient instructions to his family about his affairs.

He'd considered terminating his journey in Los Angeles because he thought it would be better to die there than in Bolivia because it would be easier to bring his body back to Australia. He considered the importance of what we were about to film and, out of consideration for me, he decided to say nothing, believing I didn't need any further complications. He would simply proceed.

He told me he had said a prayer: 'Jesus, I am doing all this travel and work for you. You determine whether I live or die. I am going to continue on this trip. It is up to you.'

When we met with Katya on Thursday 3 June 1999, she told us that Jesus had been speaking to her, telling her about the stigmata and its purpose. Katya then added, 'Jesus also told me to tell Ron there is nothing wrong with him. What he must do is learn to breathe; take a course of aspirin; rest.'

Ron found it a little hard to believe Katya could come up with a health recipe that the doctor couldn't, but she'd come up with so many surprising things in the past that Ron was inclined to do what he was told. More than anything, he was surprised that Jesus would be directing His attention towards him on such an important day.

Katya allowed me to take a blood sample from her using a syringe, which was quite an effort for me as I'm very squeamish about such things. If there was going to be a stigmata the next day, we would take samples of that blood too. There was a fascinating question regarding whose blood would be coming out of the stigmata wounds. I'd asked Katya whose blood she thought might come out of her wounds.

'Jesus',' she said, in an emotional voice.

Our group left Katya's house and drove to a restaurant. As the others went inside, I pulled Ron back and asked him what he thought about his medical advice from Jesus. Ron indicated that he didn't know what to make of it, so with only the two of us left on the street, I started on the first point.

'Ron, how do you breathe?' I asked.

He looked at me as if it were a strange question and pointed at his lips.

'Well, through my mouth,' he said.

'Well, that's just where your breath goes in and out. Where does it go?'

Ron indicated the top of his chest.

Having spent a lot of time learning how to breathe correctly in my various sporting pursuits, I knew that the majority of us breathe inadequately, in a very shallow fashion. If you don't breathe properly, you don't get the oxygen your body requires. As silly as it may sound, I soon had Ron working on emptying his body of breath completely if he could, then inhaling as deeply as he could.

We joined the rest of the party and shared a pleasant meal. Ron ate his fill. When we left the restaurant, our assigned car was a pick-up truck, and most of us had to sit in the open tray at the back. Somebody automatically opened the front passenger door for our patient, Ron, but he ignored the invitation and, with one hand on the side of the tray, jumped into the back. We were all amazed. Ron was laughing. Was this massive improvement in his health due to the supernatural powers of God? I am certain Ron thought so, though I was a little less convinced. Although Ron did not go to a doctor, for any reason, for at least ten years afterwards.

When we returned to Katya's house after dinner that night, she initially seemed fine. But as time passed, she became distracted and introspective. She quietly left us and after a while we found her in her private prayer room. She was crying. She told us that it always happened like this. That this was the worst part of the whole experience.

'Even if I am with many people, I feel lonely and abandoned, like I am not understood. I feel weak, like I cannot do anything.'

She said that Jesus had told her that nobody believed He actually sweated blood in the Garden of Gethsemane on the night before His crucifixion, where the Bible says He suffered much mental anxiety ahead of His fate. Katya's distress that night seemed to me to be mirroring that. Her suffering seemed real and profound, but of course this proved nothing. We had to wait to see what tomorrow would bring.

The following morning, we set up two cameras in Katya's bedroom, along with the big lights and reflectors. Everything was perfect – we would catch it all. We had been told that the stigmata would start at midday.

Katya was in bed wearing a blue floral nightie. I looked at her hands and there was nothing to see. The top of each foot revealed faint dark marks, which apparently were the scars of previous experiences of the stigmata.

I sat myself down next to her bed, near her head, and we waited.

Over the next few hours, Katya tossed and turned, her discomfort obvious. Her spiritual advisor, Father Renzo Sessolo, wearing his priestly collar under a grey jumper, knelt by her bed to comfort her.

I had got some advice from pathologists on how to take blood samples and store them securely. We wanted to examine everything. So the pathology gadgets added to the clutter of the humble little room, as ten or so witnesses stood around waiting while Katya suffered quietly and the clock edged slowly towards noon.

I was sitting right there, waiting, watching, when, at 12 o'clock, Father Renzo noticed them first – tiny spots of blood on her forehead. I felt a shot of adrenaline burst through my torso. The camera barely picked up the spots. But we had pictures. There was the thrill of the journalistic scoop that I'd been getting ever since I was a kid on newspapers in Perth – I wasn't going back to the office empty-handed. And then there was the awe that if this was real – and it was still a very big 'if' – I was in the presence of God.

I kept having to remind myself not to be carried away by this. Not to be that reporter at the miracle waterfall in New Zealand. I had to remain the dispassionate observer.

Another spot appeared, and another, and another. The crown of thorns.

Katya said something in Spanish.

'She feels it burning,' Father Renzo translated.

At 12.15 pm, Katya turned her left hand over. In it, she was clutching a small white crucifix on a white ribbon. There was blood on her hand. A tiny cross appeared in blood on the back of her left hand. Wounds started appearing on the top of her feet, just below her middle toes. I donned a pair of white rubber gloves and pulled out some sterile cotton buds to swab the large bloody patches. By 1 pm, the wounds had got deeper. A bruise and a graze appeared below her left eye. I continued taking swabs, as she made noises of obvious distress.

'I'm sorry, Katya,' I said, trying to be as soothing as I could while dabbing the cotton buds into her flesh. 'Just one more.'

Her wounds were deep now. Perhaps close to a centimetre. Right there, in front of my eyes. The camera was getting close-ups. It seemed very real, and I've got to say, quite upsetting.

We got all the samples we needed, so made way for some friends who had come to wrap her hands and feet in white bandages. But Katya's distress only grew worse. She moaned and writhed on the bed.

'My lungs are filling up with liquid,' she said in Spanish at about 2.45 pm.

A doctor who had seen her like this once before had told us that the first time he saw it, he thought she was dying at this point. Apparently, when you're crucified, your lungs fill with fluid, and you drown. Katya's daughter and another woman were wrapping their arms around her torso, lifting her up and forcibly getting her to breathe out and in because she couldn't do it by herself.

The distress was infectious. It affected everyone in the room as she gulped for air.

Her usually plump face now seemed thin. All colour had left it. Her eyes were rolled back. If I didn't know what was going on, I would have sworn she was dying too.

Then her breathing started to ease, and suddenly became normal.

'It's over,' Father Renzo said.

It was very disturbing. There was no way this was self-inflicted. We had been with her the whole time and we saw the wounds develop from nothing: from pink dots to gaping holes.

We sat there for a while, not sure what to do next.

'She's got to recover,' Father Renzo said. 'Nothing else is going to happen. I want you to leave her alone.'

We stayed for about an hour. I don't know what I was waiting for, but if there was some sort of hoax being pulled, I just felt I had to stick with it for a while longer. Eventually, I turned to Katya and told her we were leaving.

'Do you want to have lunch tomorrow?'

'Yes, please,' she replied weakly.

And so we left. We had it all on film. It was an experience that will never go away from me. It was very, very powerful. Especially for a non-believer like myself. All I really wanted to do at this point was get back to my room and sit in silence to contemplate what I'd just seen.

Anybody who knows me well knows that I need to do this on a regular basis. I need to sit alone with a cigar and just let thoughts wash over me. It's what my crew saw me do in Vietnam on the two occasions when I dodged death. It's what my family see me do on the most mundane of days. I need that time alone to think.

I got to my room, took out a cigar and I ruminated. I knew that reporting what I had just seen would open me to ridicule from journalist colleagues and the sceptical commentariat. They'd say that Katya or one of her entourage had found a way to secretly inflict the wounds without me noticing. I knew it was possible that I'd been fooled by some sleight of hand, but I couldn't see how. I'd seen those drops of blood appear spontaneously, one by one. And what about the two cameras? Surely they would have picked it up. We'd have to study the tapes

Signs from God

closely. The bleeding by itself would be easy enough to fake, but those wounds were real. I'd put the swabs *into* them.

On a professional level, I knew that I wouldn't have to do much for the show. I'd just broadcast the footage and let the pictures speak for themselves. But on a personal level, the whole thing was very difficult for me. I couldn't rationalise it in my mind. I knew what I'd seen – and I believed it was authentic.

My confidence started to shake. From that day on, I would no longer be able to say, 'I don't believe in God.' Instead, I would have to say, 'I don't know if there is a God. I've seen some powerful evidence that there is, but I don't know how authentic it is to say it came from God.'

Almost as important as witnessing the stigmata was going back the next day to examine the wounds. I'd been told that in the past, Katya's wounds had healed by the day after the stigmata. If the *wounds* could be explained away as psychosomatic, could such instant *healing* also be explained as a case of mind over matter? That would be some mind.

When we arrived back at Katya's house, down the potholed street with cows wandering around, she was still in bed in the blue nightie. She was smiling weakly like someone on the mend from an illness.

'Good morning, *buenos dias*, Mike,' she greeted me.

I kissed her lightly on each cheek.

Less than 24 hours earlier she appeared to be dying and here she was almost fully recovered. I was stunned by the change in her.

'I can't go to lunch,' she said. 'I just don't feel well enough.'

But she did let us examine her wounds. Those below her left eye had disappeared, as had the marks on her forehead.

The gaping wounds on her hands were gone, replaced by what looked like a shallow bruise and a small closed cut. The spot where the holes in her feet had been looked more like recently healed wounds, but smooth to the touch, with no scabs. Just little lines running in towards the centre. If you'd asked me, I would have thought the wounds were about a fortnight old.

Katya said she received a message from Jesus after her suffering. She pulled out her ox blood-coloured book and read: 'I have been preparing you for this day because I needed to reach the world one more time through someone like you to show the world my suffering. Thank you.'

We still had the blood to test. First, it was just to check that it was blood, but more profoundly, it was to ask the question: if the wounds are the wounds of Christ, will the blood be the blood of Christ? Fox wanted a live element to the show, so those results were going be held over until the show went to air. I had to wait a couple of months before I got an answer to that enormous question.

The whole experience had been challenging for me personally. I had to make up my own mind about what I believed after witnessing Katya's stigmata. That question was no longer just something I would be asking viewers. It was now a question I needed to answer for myself. After all this time, did I now believe in God?

Nineteen

Showing the World

We produced a 90-minute special called *Signs From God* which aired in the US on 28 July 1999. Fox brought in a very professional presenter by the name of Giselle Fernández to front the show. She was a serious network reporter who'd covered the first Gulf War for CBS, won five Emmy Awards for journalism, and had even scored an international scoop when she interviewed the media-shy Fidel Castro. In the broadcast, I was more the on-the-road reporter.

It opened spectacularly, with Giselle bursting onto the slick stage in a black suit and heals, addressing the viewers: 'On the cusp of a new century, a new millennium, the world is experiencing an unprecedented wave of reports of supernatural happenings. People are insisting they are being given divine messages. Important messages. And in many cases their claims appear to be supported by extraordinary events. Tonight we expose a range of these claims to science. And as we take you live around the world in our search for answers and subject these reported signs from God to thorough expert analysis, we invite you, the viewer, to take your place in the jury . . .'

The program put a lot of emphasis on an increasing tide of natural disasters and played up the millennial angle.

And then Giselle introduced me. 'The show you are about to watch was seven years in the making. It is about people who did not in any way seek our attention. And it is about an internationally respected journalist who won their trust and found himself being changed in the process. His name is Michael Willesee. I understand from all the work you've done over the years where you are renowned for your scepticism and investigative abilities, this is not only different, this project we're about to see has been extraordinary for you.'

Seated on the wood-panelled set in Los Angeles, I explained the way Ron had brought me in to have a look as an outsider.

'A lot has happened since then. It's been an extraordinary journey.'

We discussed Katya's background and I emphasised her lack of education and the fact that she'd produced nine books, some of which she'd written in Polish and Greek.

'Specifically, I said, "How can you write in Greek when you don't even know the characters?" And she said, quite simply, "Jesus shows me these characters."'

'Okay,' Giselle responded, 'we've set the scene, but we've got a lot of viewers out there who are watching and who are already sceptical. What do you say to them?'

'Look, I understand exactly where they're coming from. I was there. I was very sceptical, but I would suggest they hold fire, at least until the next segment, where we do test Katya, and the results are stunning.'

The program then covered Katya's EEG and the surprising conversation that Katya seemed to have with Doctor Pelle. When I told Giselle about the hairs standing up on the back of my neck, she asked if it was a turning point for me in my research.

'It made me think very, very seriously,' I answered.

We brought on Father Peter Stravinskas, editor of the *Catholic Answer*, who expressed interest in what he'd seen, along with a healthy dose of doubt.

'The Lord tells us several times in the Gospels, "An evil generation seeks a sign." In other words, we're supposed to be able to believe without external evidence or supernatural phenomena. The Lord appears to St Thomas a week after His resurrection and says, "Blessed are they who have belief, but who have not seen." That having been said, once a person alleges to have had some sort of mystical supernatural experience, the Church believe that such a thing is possible, but highly improbable. It's possible it's from God. It's possible it's from the Devil. It's possible that it's from a sick mind. Or even worse perhaps, someone who is engaged in fraud.'

Sitting there in the studio, I responded, 'Father, I've got to say your answer confuses me because Jesus Himself was a man of great signs. Fatima was about signs. Padre Pio who was recently beatified was a stigmatist. He was about signs. So what you say confuses me.'

'The presumption is that these extraordinary phenomena are not the way God normally works to communicate His will or His way,' explained Father Stravinskas. 'Jesus became very, very upset when people conditioned belief, demanded particular signs in order to believe. God is the Lord of nature, and as the Lord of nature, He normally prefers to work through nature. He can suspend the laws of nature in order to communicate an extraordinary message or to get mankind's attention.'

Giselle then interviewed Ricardo Castanon, live from Cochabamba. She got right to the point.

'I imagine you come across a lot of frauds in your work. How many do you find to be genuine?'

'I have studied around 50 cases on four continents. And from them, six cases were false. It is not as some people say that every one is false. I think before we talk and we say, "I am a sceptic" or "I don't believe this", we must go very deep with this information to know whether it is truth or not.'

'Of the ones you've deemed authentic, what do they have in common, if anything?' Giselle asked.

'We get the technical results, but normally we have to study the life of these people. They are people who try to have a holy life, they are humble, they are not looking for money. When I am studying cases in America, the first question is "Did they get money or not?" These people lead a very quiet life. They pray a lot. They want to help pilgrims. They want to help people.

'But I have to say also, that it's also important to know as a warning that some people were authentic for some years but because of their human weaknesses, they were not able to keep a holy life. They changed and they wanted money, copyright. They said the messages belonged to them. Then they didn't have a holy life. And that is why the Church is very prudent not only to say whether they are authentic or not but whether they keep a holy life.'

'Doctor Castanon, you were once an atheist,' I said. 'What has happened to the certainty that you had that God did not exist?'

He explained that he wanted to study these phenomena as an atheist 'to give some orientation to the people. Because it's very easy to say, "It's true maybe. Or maybe not." It's important to say the truth to people. And the truth showed me that these miracles are happening and now I believe in this spirit.'

We cut to a live shot of a 'bleeding' statue in Bolivia. Back when we'd turned up to film the statue for the show, nothing had happened. To me, it was still just a statue with some disfiguring dark material on it. Nevertheless, we had Ron's footage of it bleeding and crying, and we had some of the caked-on 'blood' to test.

It was the first major forensic challenge for the show. Where were these tears coming from? And what about the 'blood'? Did it have DNA? If so, whose? What would that reveal?

The first place to look was in the bust itself. We took it to a *laboratoria* for a CAT scan. If there was a pinprick as thick as a human hair, we would be able to find it. It was placed into the glowing white cylinder. By the time we brought it out, the technicians were in agreement: there was no device or aperture in it. As this footage ran, I said in the voiceover, 'Science has no explanation for the weeping or bleeding.'

Then it was time to test the blood on the tortured face.

We had a forensic scientist, Lisa Calandro, lined up to go live. She worked with many of California's various police departments in DNA analysis in her job with the company Forensic Analytical in Oakland, California. She explained how they treated my sample like they would any other.

'First, we examined it visually and it was a very small – approximately half-centimetre squared – dried crust with some red material on it. We subjected that material to a chemical test for the presence of blood and from there we characterised the blood to determine whether or not it was human.'

'And what did you find?' Giselle asked.

'That it was human blood. We subsequently used DNA-testing methods to determine that the blood originated from a female.'

Giselle turned to me across the desk at which we were sitting.

'That leaves the question for you Mike: they found human, female blood on the statue. What does that tell us?'

This was all happening live, so I didn't have time to think. In hindsight, I should have just told her that it was most likely to be DNA left behind by one of the many women who had handled the statue in recent years because the previous three DNA tests done by government laboratories had found no human genetic material.

But instead I got a bit more imaginative.

'It doesn't tell me anything,' I said. 'I could hazard a guess, but I stress it's just a guess. If you believe in the theory of the immaculate conception, Jesus had a mother, but no father. If He is of the flesh of His mother. Could Jesus be of the blood of His mother?'

'That is perhaps one of the most creative theories I've heard in a long time,' Giselle said. All smiles. 'Perhaps it wouldn't stand up in a court of law, but we're reminded that the statue put in a CAT scan revealed no sign of tampering whatsoever. I guess we have to keep on testing.'

We then crossed straight to the home of Ermila 'Mila' Carrasco, the grandmother from Mexico.

'This is where it all started,' I explained. 'In one small house in Monterrey in Mexico, we heard reports of a religious image appearing through a concrete floor, a picture of the Virgin Mary that shed tears before a variety of witnesses, and rose petals somehow revealing religious images. This was indeed an opportunity to see, to touch, to test.

'How would you react if you were mopping the floor and an image started to appear?' I went on. 'And you can't remove it? In fact, as Mila started to scrub, the image actually became stronger. It appears to be of our Lady of Guadalupe, the most famous religious icon of Latin America.'

Signs from God

We showed pictures of Mila mopping the floor and the silhouette of a face, with the very pronounced rays of light emanating out from behind it in neat symmetry.

When my crew and I arrived at Mila's house, we'd witnessed an extraordinary happening – and we'd got it on film. This was the footage that ran next.

On a picture of the Virgin Mary that was kept between two sheets of glass, a drop like a tear appeared.

'The important thing about this image,' I explained to camera, 'the two pieces of glass are sandwiched together. There is no room for any device which could fabricate weeping.'

I turned it around and the audience could see there was no backing. It was totally translucent.

Then it was time for the rose petals. I held two petals in my hand, both showing an image which appeared to be that of a person with a covered head, praying. They were very similar, yet at the same time, clearly different.

For the live-cross to Mila's house, a young reporter who was fluent in Spanish had placed a number of large petals into a Bible she had brought along.

'If anything happens to these rose petals, we'll be right here to show you,' she said.

We had to test the images on the petals, and Fox wanted everything to be immediate, live. It created challenges.

One of our experts was Will Shank, an art conservator who worked for museums in London, Madrid and the United States. His primary job was to preserve and protect some of the world's great art treasures, so he needed to have an intimate knowledge of how such works were made.

He was, understandably, sceptical about the origins of our miniature masterpieces.

'But I'm also a believer in phenomena that can't be explained rationally,' he said. 'And I was hoping that this might be one of those cases. I am, however, an analytical kind of guy.'

'Did you believe, automatically, that these are the work of man?' Giselle asked him.

'Automatically, that's what suggested itself to me, but I wanted to get as much information as I could about how they were made.'

He photographed one of Mila's petals with a strong light behind it and blew up the image to about A4-sized. He noted that the images were not random maybe-it-is-maybe-it-isn't type images. They were clearly replicas of iconic pictures.

He also examined a petal itself and determined that there was no paint or other foreign marking on it, and that the parts of the petal with the image were much thinner than the rest of the petal. He looked at it with a strong light from the side, showing the valleys and peaks, and said they suggested that something had been pressed into the petal. He also found what he thought was a fingerprint around the image, which was likely caused by pressing hard into the petal, not casual handling of it.

As part of his investigation, Shank had tried to recreate such images on rose petals.

'With the help of friends and colleagues, I experimented with everything I thought might be available in a modest dwelling in Mexico without any sophisticated technology. I tried heat, I tried acids in the form of lime juice, I tried bases in the form of household bleach.'

And he also used *milagros*, the little metal folk charms that are commonly used in Mexico for healing and as offerings to gain favour. He heated one up and pressed it into a rose petal. And it came up with an impressive image, to be sure, but it didn't actually look like any of Mila's. It was much darker with harder outlines. Mila's petals were exquisite, subtle almost to perfection, and they'd endured for years. Whereas the test samples looked like they'd been rudely stamped. And it was not given the opportunity to stand the test of time. I had so many questions, but we were on a schedule and we didn't have time.

Giselle asked me what I thought.

'This is part of the testing process,' I said. 'It doesn't completely answer it. Let's go to the botanists.'

We had a botanist, Doctor Michael Reid, a Kiwi with a bald head and white lab coat, standing by at the University of California, Davis. Giselle asked him about the fragility of petals.

'I was intrigued by the images, Giselle, but I would say that rose petals are not that delicate. We all know about people wearing roses at balls and parties and rose petals being thrown through the air. In fact, rose petals have a surface that's like a very flexible skin, like plastic.'

Like our previous expert, he thought that pressing the petals was the most likely way to achieve such an image. He then pressed a medallion into a petal with his thumb.

'Then I could look at it in a microscope and see pretty much the same sort of pattern that was seen in Mila's pictures.'

He showed us his renderings and, really, they were more in the category of those pieces of toast or misshapen carrots. You couldn't see much. He had nothing further to add.

We crossed live to Mila, who maintained that the petals were signs from God. It was a frustrating process for me. I had so much more I wanted to do and say. But it was live and we had to move on.

At last it was time to go to our show's centrepiece, Katya's stigmata. We started with a potted history of the stigmata, how it went back to St Francis of Assisi, who, in 1224, became the first recorded Christian to have suffered wounds replicating those of Christ, and how just before *Signs From God* went to air, a more recent stigmatist, a priest by the name of Padre Pio, was beatified by the Pope in front of a crowd of a million people. The Vatican had only verified 12 such cases, and I pondered whether Katya might turn out to be the thirteenth.

The footage of Katya's stigmata started running, and, as she went through the profound difficulties on the night before, Giselle asked me how confident I had been that we were actually going to see anything the next day and whether her symptoms could be psychosomatic. It was a good question.

'There are doctors, psychiatrists, even priests, who believe the external signs of the stigmata can be psychosomatic. So if Katya was somehow mentally inducing all this, then her distress the night before could not be seen as conclusive proof of the stigmata to come.'

We went on to show Katya's experience in all its extraordinary detail, and as it drew to a close, Giselle turned to me and commented on how difficult it was to watch.

'How did you react, being there and watching it with your own eyes?'

'It was very disturbing. I think a lot of the viewers watching now will feel what I felt then. Maybe being there was a little bit worse.'

'Mind-blowing,' she said. 'Yet many of those viewers you talk about will be sitting there thinking it's totally self-inflicted. Was there any point where you saw her, or she could have done this to herself?'

'There is no way that was self-inflicted. We were there with her all the time. We saw the wounds start from nothing. The first wound on her hand was a little dot and you saw the end result.'

'You're a sceptical journalist. Are you feeling a bit more spiritual these days after watching that first-hand?'

'It certainly pushes you heavily in that direction.'

I made my point about the speed of healing being important to rule out the possibility of the wounds being psychosomatic. But I pointed out to Giselle that the blood test results were a fascinating element that we were now awaiting. First, to figure out whose blood it was, but second, to maybe answer that enormous question: 'If the wounds are the wounds of Christ, could the blood be the blood of Christ?'

'I'm glad we're not asking any small questions in our special,' she joked.

We threw back to forensic DNA expert Lisa Calandro in her lab. And somewhat anticlimactically she confirmed that the blood taken from Katya's wounds was Katya's.

Giselle asked me if I was disappointed.

I said I didn't feel let down.

'The blood results were normal; it was just the filming that was extraordinary. How could you be disappointed with film like that? If we looked for too much in the blood, we didn't get it. In the filming, we got the extraordinary.'

The program then went off on a pre-millennium tangent about natural disasters apparently increasing in the lead up to 2000, and brought back the commentator, Father Peter Stravinskas, who said they were perhaps a wake-up call, a simple reminder, like all the miracles that had occurred during the last century of the millennium, to heed the fundamental message of the Gospels.

I broke in, 'Father, what's your reaction to the apparent stigmata of Katya?'

'My approach would still be extremely cautious. The Church has procedures for reacting to these alleged very extraordinary phenomena, and from what I can gather those procedures have been followed very carefully in this case. There is still, as far as I know, no definitive acceptance of the supernatural character. I think it's also important to point out to our viewers that while the Church might approve an apparition or some kind of supernatural phenomenon, it does not require Catholics to believe in those phenomena, even if approved. They're declared worthy of belief which is to say a Catholic is free to believe in it if he chooses but need not do so.'

After the ad break, we went to my formal interview with Katya, which we'd recorded before the stigmata. I was in suit and tie, she was in her Sunday best, with a little make-up. I started by asking her what Jesus looked like when He appeared to her during our EEG testing.

'Beautiful,' she said. 'He was wearing a white tunic with a robe, smiling. His eyes were very light. Very beautiful . . . Beautiful.'

'Katya, tell me what you saw when you were looking over my shoulder.'

'Above your head, Mike, when you were asking me how He looks, He was smiling right behind you so that I could describe Him to you.'

'Is He there now?'

'*Si*.'

'Do you want to talk with Him?'

'I don't need to.'

'Katya, is this the first time you've seen Jesus like this?'

'Yes, that I see His full figure.'

'He was there, as if there was a man there?'

'*Si*.'

It was a long interview, touching on many subjects and it's a great shame that we had to cut so much. At one point, I asked her what sins most offended Jesus. She responded by saying that all sins were an offence to God.

'There is no such thing as a big lie or a small lie. It is a lie. There is no such thing as a big theft or a small theft, it is theft. But I think the thing that hurts Jesus the most is arrogance.'

'Katya, of all the messages you've received, if you had to make one simple summary of them, what would it be?'

'That He is always waiting for His children. And that when we say yes to Him, He is very prodigal with His love and mercy.'

'Katya, were you seeing Jesus when you were telling me that?'

She nodded. 'He was speaking to me about His love and mercy.'

'Does He have anything else to say?'

'That He expects that each one of these words will fall like dew drops . . .' Here, she paused for quite a long time. 'To comfort and mend hearts . . . because the world is full of pain and suffering.'

At that point I noticed her eyes were again up over my shoulder. 'You keep looking,' I said.

'He says that He is looking at you, Mike, and He is blessing the work that you are doing. He says that these words are for you also.'

While we were editing this footage, one of our editors had noticed a strange reflection in Katya's left eye. We decided to computer enhance her eyes to get a closer look. There was no doubt that the light reflecting off the right part of her eyeball appeared to have got brighter.

I explained this to the viewers in the voiceover.

'It's definitely brighter,' I said. 'I don't know what's causing it, but there's a lot more definition in the reflection.

There's nothing that's changed in the set up, but whatever it's reflecting is definitely stronger.'

Was it Jesus? Unfortunately, that was one question that we couldn't find an expert to answer.

'The judgment must be yours,' I told the viewers in my voiceover.

Katya was watching the program live in Cochabamba and we crossed to her for the final minutes. She and Giselle had a brief conversation in Spanish before I asked her what she thought of the show. It had to be translated into Spanish and back again, so it was slow for live television. But she approved. I asked if she had a message from Jesus.

'Yes, I do have a message and I will read it right now.

'"Dear Man of the 20th century, you have forgotten me. I will be coming back again, to take you away from the darkness and show you the true faith. I come to help you. I want to put my heart next to your heart, to translate my love to all humanity. Do you want to help me? Your souls are as delicate as a rose petal. Let me impress in it my love."'

'Katya, a lot of people are watching the program tonight. What do you want them to take away from it?'

'I want them to remember that we have a live Christ in the Eucharist, that Jesus is waiting for us, and please don't forget Jesus' suffering for all of us.'

As Giselle and I shook hands at the end, she asked me for my final thoughts.

'It's changed me,' I said, 'and I hope it gives people a lot to think about.'

It had changed me. But while I might have given viewers the impression that I'd swallowed the whole enchilada, I hadn't. I still did not consider myself a believer. I'd seen some amazing things, things that I could find no explanation for except the existence of some external, unknowable force, but seeing such things did not convert me. Looking back at it now, I'm not sure why not. But they didn't. Perhaps because I knew I still had so much to do.

Part Six

The Journey Continues

Twenty

What Next?

When *Signs From God* was in post-production, getting ready to go to air, David Hill had taken a week off to go fishing. In his absence, a cabal of people who didn't share his vision for the show were in charge and they took our promos off the air. He had come back a few days before we went to air and put the promos straight back on, but we feared it was too late. We didn't have as much buzz around the show as we would have liked, and we worried that a lot of people who might be interested in our subject would not even know it was on.

After it aired, we nervously awaited the ratings numbers. When they came in, they knocked our socks off. Twenty-eight million people had watched. These were extraordinary numbers. You have to be the Super Bowl or the Oscars to beat that sort of number.

We were also awaiting the critical response to the show. To be honest, I've never worried much about what critics think. Their job is to be critical – and interesting. They've got to have something to say, so let them say it. To me, it's always been about the ratings. I do care about ratings. That's the proof of whether what you're doing is worthy or not – whether you can hold the attention of the average viewer.

It wasn't surprising that I copped a bit. Some people said I'd dropped my guard, that I'd lost my famous scepticism. That I'd been duped by fraudsters. Of course Katya's wounds were self-inflicted, they said. She obviously had something hidden beneath the sheets.

But I'd sat there and watched those pinpricks appear on her forehead out of nowhere. I'd dabbed my swabs deep into her flesh and we had it all on video. Nobody came up with a genuine criticism. In fact, there were fewer criticisms than I expected, because they were not just having to take a journalist's word on the events – it was all there on tape.

From a professional point of view, I was pretty happy with what I'd done. In my 30 years in television, it was the first time I'd made a show specifically for the American market and I'd slayed it. We were even sent a Florida newspaper clipping about a famous American footballer who converted after seeing the show.

We started receiving a lot of letters, but Fox didn't seem to be revelling in our success the way we thought they would. For example, we had been forwarded 1000 letters from Fox's Florida office, but not a single letter from the California head office. We knew the letters were being sent, but Fox California wasn't passing them on. I had assumed that the network would be all over us, trying to get a sequel out of us off the back of our runaway success, but they were strangely silent.

As it turned out, there was something of a palace coup going on and our great backer, David Hill, found himself being pushed sideways. His shows were under threat.

Network politics, however, were not at the forefront of my mind. There was something of a palace coup going on in my

The Journey Continues

own consciousness and the way I perceived the world. While I hadn't converted, I was grappling with this new notion of God. But the old me still needed to know if it was true or false. He needed evidence. He needed tests.

All I had at that point was a conviction that what had happened to Katya was true. That fuelled the idea that we could do further testing on other claims. Ron certainly wasn't stopping. And nor was I.

Six weeks after *Signs From God* had aired in the United States, Ricardo Castanon got in touch: he had a new case and he asked Ron to travel to Argentina to look into it with him.

The case had started three years earlier, on 18 August 1996, in a parish called Santa Maria, in the downtown area of the Argentine capital, Buenos Aires. Priest Alejandro Pezet had conducted Mass and an elderly parishioner, Emma Fernandez, was helping tidy up afterwards. Fernandez was a 'Eucharistic minister', a layperson with the authority and the blessing to administer Holy Communion. Around 7 pm, she found a dirty communion host that had been discarded in a candle holder. This sort of thing happened from time to time. Perhaps a parishioner had dropped it on the floor and then did not want to swallow it, so had quietly dumped it. To the Church, a consecrated host is very special; you can't just throw away the flesh of Christ. Fernandez showed Father Pezet the dirty communion host. Often in such a situation, the priest will simply eat the host himself, but this one was quite dusty so instead, Father Pezet instructed Emma Fernandez to put the host in a crystal bowl used for baptisms. She put the bowl in the back corner of the tabernacle where it was expected to dissolve, after which it could be disposed of correctly – by pouring the water onto a plant.

Eight days later, before the 8 am Mass on Monday 26 August, Fernandez went to see if the host had dissolved. She pulled out the bowl and was surprised by what she found. The wafer no longer looked like a wafer. It had turned red. It looked like blood. She hurried to show Father Pezet, who was praying nearby.

'Father, something strange is going on in that host you had me put in the tabernacle.'

He peered into the bowl and saw what looked like blood. He at once thought that perhaps something supernatural was going on, and so informed the auxiliary bishop, Jorge Bergoglio, who ordered that the host be professionally photographed. The photographer, Marcelo Antonini, took pictures of the host that very day, after which it was returned to the tabernacle.

Tabernacles are designed to lock, in order to keep the Eucharist secure from unauthorised hands. This tabernacle was no exception, and therefore was beyond the reach of interference. When the photographer returned 12 days later, his excellent pictures clearly showed that the blood-like substance on the host was increasing in size – barely a hint of the wafer's original outline remained.

The specimen was locked backed into a different tabernacle in the sacristy – the room out the back where various sacred vessels and parish records are kept – where it remained a strict secret for three years. During that time, it appeared to suffer no decomposition. When Bergoglio became the archbishop, he instructed that the host be investigated more thoroughly. And that's where Doctor Ricardo Castanon came into the picture.

Ricardo explained to Ron and me that he had happened to be in Buenos Aires on other business with Katya at the time. He had actually taken her with him when he went to examine this mysterious host. While she was looking at it, Katya said that Jesus told her, 'I want Doctor Castanon to take charge of this case because through it I want to bring back dignity to my altar.'

After Ron joined him in Buenos Aires this time around, they interviewed all the eyewitnesses they could lay their hands on, from the woman who'd found the host, to the priest and the photographer. They all seemed touched by the experience. When it came time to take a sample from the host, Archbishop Bergoglio had organised a separate camera crew so there were two cameras filming from each side of the table.

Knowing that such claims had been dismissed in the past, Ron and Ricardo put a lot of effort into ensuring the chain of evidence was kept tight and well documented. A sample of the host was placed in a test tube, which was then packed and sealed into a container, with their signatures across the tape that secured it.

Ron knew from the pictures that were taken in the early days that the whitish round shape of the communion host had morphed into the red substance over time. Because in the early progression of photos, you could still see the outline of the host, gradually being replaced. This showed that nobody had simply swapped out the host for this red substance.

I soon joined the team and we set out to do what we thought would be a straightforward process – get the best labs in the world to take a look at this reddish material and tell us what it was. If there was DNA, we wanted to know what it was; perhaps even *whose* it was.

Ron flew the sample from Buenos Aires to San Francisco for testing, dropping into Texas on the way to see Katya, who was giving a talk there. When Ron went to see her, she told him that Jesus had a message for him.

'You have no idea how important the work you are doing is,' the message started. 'You are going to encounter difficulties, but don't be perturbed. Don't think I'm going to allow you to be abandoned if your interests are the same as my interests.'

It was something that Ron was able to hold on to for the next 20 years as we encountered difficulty after difficulty. He never felt abandoned.

Ron took the sample to Forensic Analytical, the same lab we'd used in *Signs From God*. They examined it and found no blood. They did find human DNA but failed to get a genetic profile from it.

This turned out to be a pattern that was repeated over and over. And I'd go so far as to say it was one of the most serious obstacles I've ever faced in my journalistic career. The laboratories would advise us that the sample appeared to be in good order so the tests would be straightforward. They would tell us to return in a few days for the results. But we would go back and there would be no response, no answer. A couple of times we were told that it was human blood, but that they could not find any DNA. They'd apologise and we'd be out on the street with nothing.

We tried to find people of high standing in the scientific world to approach and ask to conduct the tests for us. But many would pull out once they realised that we were on a quest to test the truth of alleged miracles. There's something about miracles that makes scientific people shrink away. Their sense of curiosity seems to abandon them when they come across events that are spectacularly curious. I couldn't really blame them – after all, I'd felt the same way myself until recently.

Twenty-one

Things Science Can't Explain

The first reported case of a bleeding host goes back 1200 years, to Lanciano, Italy, where a monk was about to offer Mass. The identity of the monk is unknown, but a document from 1631 described him as 'not very firm in the faith, versed in the sciences of the world, but ignorant in that of God'.

Apparently plagued by doubts about whether it really was the blood and flesh of Christ that he was handing out to his flock, he nevertheless continued on. But this time, as he consecrated the host it changed into flesh and the wine turned to blood. The monk was enthralled. Weeping, he called the congregation in to see it.

'Oh fortunate witnesses, to whom the Blessed God, to confound my unbelief, has wished to reveal Himself visible to our eyes!'

Since then, the Church has declared such transformed communion hosts to be miraculous more than 100 times.

But it wasn't until 1971 that Professor Odoardo Linoli conducted the first scientific examination of these inexplicable occurrences. The professor in anatomy and pathological histology ran the 1200-year-old Lanciano specimen through a series of tests. In something of a first, he published his findings in a peer-reviewed scientific journal, *Quaderni Sclavo di Diagnostica Clinica e di Laboratorio*. The blood was typed as AB, which is rare in Italy, but almost three times more common in Israel. He found no trace of any preservative that might have kept the specimen whole for 1200 years. But it was when he looked at it under the microscope that it got really interesting.

'I examined the flesh and found it was myocardium (heart muscle),' he told Ron and me, almost 30 years later, through a translator. 'I also found veins and arteries typical of the inner part of the heart, so it was heart for sure.'

He didn't need any convincing that this was the heart tissue of Jesus Christ. The Church was elated with his findings. I asked him how he felt when he first saw the results of his tests.

'I felt as if I was floating 35 centimetres above the ground.'

Because we kept hitting a brick wall with the DNA testing, we decided we needed to look at our sample in the same way Professor Linoli had looked at his – through a microscope. For that, we needed a pathologist.

The people at Forensic Analytical referred us on to top-line Californian forensic pathologist Doctor Robert Lawrence and forwarded our samples to him. Once he had prepared the sample and taken a thin slice for a microscope slide, Ron and I went to visit him.

The son of a famous nuclear physicist, Doctor Lawrence was deeply rooted in the scientific tradition. He seemed like a smart guy. Lawrence explained that he had been doing autopsies on bodies that had died unnatural deaths for the past 27 years. He had examined more than 7000 bodies, many of which had died violently. He'd given evidence in court many hundreds of times. Usually for the prosecution.

We did not tell him the purpose of our quest. But soon after introducing ourselves, I asked him, 'Do you have any idea why we're here?'

'Well, from what I've seen of your sample, and the fact that a lawyer and a journalist have flown all the way from Australia to get my opinion, I have to presume it's a high-profile case and could have to do with the death of a high-profile person.'

He wasn't wrong.

Once Doctor Lawrence had examined the prepared slides of the substance from the Buenos Aires host, he concluded that what he was looking at was human skin, more specifically, epidermis, the outermost layer of skin and, curiously, that it was infiltrated with white blood cells, which are the body's frontline immune defence against infection.

As he later told us in an interview: 'They were active living white cells at the time they were collected. There was some inflammatory process going on.'

Ron and I were somewhat taken aback by this conclusion. The host from which the sample was drawn was almost four years old, having been discovered in August 1996. The host had then been put in water and locked in a tabernacle for most of the intervening years before this sample had been taken from it just a few months previously. Yet Lawrence's conclusion was that the cells were active and living at the time they were put in the test tube.

We came clean on the sample's background.

He remained firm on his point. 'If this material had been placed directly into water after it had been taken off a body, I would expect these cells to be dissolved in minutes to an hour or two.'

Our next decision was to photograph the slides Lawrence had made, and to travel to Lanciano, to see Professor Linoli and get him to look at the slides and tell us what he thought.

At this time, Ron and I were travelling with Katya and with Father Mark Withoos – a priest who was a great friend of ours working in the Vatican, but who was wary of anyone making mystical claims – as well as another lawyer, Charles Morton.

A lifelong practising Catholic, on 12 December 1999, Charles had rolled the family Landcruiser on a dirt road out near Wagga Wagga in southwestern New South Wales. The car was totalled but he, his wife and their six kids walked away unscathed. A day or so after the accident, Charles heard that the Pope had just declared 12 December to be the feast day of Our Lady of Guadalupe, protector of unborn children.

A little like my response to being in the plane crash, this experience sparked a search for meaning of sorts for Charles. He got an introduction to Ron and me, and now he was here in Rome, heading down to Lanciano on a minibus with me and Ron, Katya Rivas and Father Mark Withoos.

As Charles would later recount: 'Katya walked past me and I smelt this whole plume of roses, and I said to Father Mark Withoos sitting beside me, "Can you smell those roses?" He said, "Listen, don't be fooled by that. She may have a rose atomiser." "Well, normally it wouldn't worry me, but when I had my nose operated on for polyps many years ago, I lost all sense of smell. That's the first time I've smelt roses in 18 years."'

The experience of travelling with Katya was fascinating: despite the fact that she has an association with Christ, on every other level she was just like an ordinary person. She wouldn't draw attention to herself. She'd often just quietly pull out a notebook and start writing as Jesus dictated.

Once in Lanciano, Ron and I got our meeting and asked Professor Linoli to look at the pictures of the microscopic slides of the substance on the host from Buenos Aires. He thought it looked like muscle tissue.

'This is definitely tissue,' he said. 'I can't say for sure from the picture. But this could be heart. You see, this is the tissue,' he said, pointing at the blown-up images of the microscope slides. 'These are the cells. They could be blood cells.'

So now we had Professor Linoli in Italy saying it might be heart tissue in the communion host from Buenos Aires and Doctor Lawrence saying it was skin tissue – and that something inexplicable was going on with the white blood cells. It was simultaneously intriguing and frustrating, and certainly brought home to us the limits of the scientific method. Despite science's claims of objectivity, so much of it still comes down to people and their perceptions.

Before heading to Lanciano, we had also given Doctor Lawrence the sample from Silvia Arevalo's statue that I'd taken from its forehead during the filming of *Signs From God*.

He said that it looked like a scab with a little bit of skin attached. He took us into his lab where the slide under the microscope was projected onto a larger screen. Ron asked what he could tell us about the skin.

'Well, it's epidermis. There was no deeper skin. This generally looks like dried blood that was pulled off the skin.'

I asked what part of the body it might have come from. He said that going by the thinness of the epidermis, 'It would be more delicate skin such as the facial area around the eyelids or upper lip.'

'Forehead?' I asked.

'Forehead, yes.'

He explained that a scab can only grow on a living thing.

He said that if you drop blood on your arm, you're not going to form a scab.

'So, this scab tells me that there's life in the source of the scab,' he said. 'A scab is the body's reaction to injury. This person has suffered an injury, a scab has formed and what I'm looking at looks like the scab has been pulled from the face of the person, because it's taken a part of the epidermis with it – a piece of skin.'

'What would you say if I told you it came off a statue?' I asked.

'Well, I'd say, err . . . You've got to give me more information. Was it a piece of material like a flake of paint from this statue? Or was it that the whole statue was covered in this and it was pulled off?'

'The statue has been filmed bleeding and we took a sample of what appeared to be blood, after it had cried, and it tested positive as human blood. We also put the statue through a CAT scan to see if it had been tampered with in any way. And it had not been tampered with.'

'Then I would be very interested in looking at the statue. This material would not come from an inanimate object so, therefore, the statue is either not a statue . . .'

He stopped mid-sentence, realising that it was an unusual thing to say – that the statue might not be a statue – but we knew exactly what he meant.

He regrouped and continued. 'I'm having a hard time in my mind deciding what it could be . . . I would suspect it has somehow been meddled with. That would be my thought. That someone has tampered with the statue. And the apparent bleeding was something that was coming from a contaminant . . . or there's a source dripping down on it. That would be the only explanation that springs to mind.'

The Journey Continues

I told him again that we'd filmed the blood appearing spontaneously.

He again professed his doubt. He believed that it was a trick, not dissimilar to other magic tricks he had seen, but which can ultimately be explained as not magic at all. I countered by explaining that we had full access to the statue – that we had been allowed to examine it, unrestricted.

'You're saying blood appeared from these wounds that had not been there before. Tears appeared to come from the eyes, and it was not there beforehand? It was not dripping down from above? Well, you know all I can say is that I would find that very amazing and my thought would be that it's an outstanding magic trick. I mean, I've seen elephants disappear myself. I've been right there . . . And I know that that didn't really happen. So that would be my thought. That this was a deception of some kind.'

'Except if you asked the magician to let you examine how the elephant disappeared, he would say, "No". In this case we were given full access to the statue and had control of the statue.'

'Well, that's quite interesting,' he said, followed by a pause. 'My father was a pure scientist, a nuclear physicist, a Nobel Prize winner. He invented the cyclotron which split the atom and more or less started the nuclear age that we're all experiencing today. He died in the 1950s. I wish we had him here right now. I'm sure he'd be very interested in something like this.

'I think it would be wonderful if one single supernatural or miracle type event were to be actually proven. Spectacular. I think it would be of great benefit to mankind. It would make us scientists sit on our hind legs. Make us do some rethinking.

'On the other hand,' he laughed, 'I would feel great gratification if I was somehow able to assist others in showing that this was a fraud. Either result will be very satisfying to me.'

Doctor Lawrence said that he didn't believe in God or an afterlife but would like to be proven wrong.

'I'd really like to have a look at this statue,' he said.

I thought that sounded like a good idea. We couldn't bring the statue to California, so a couple of months later, I brought Doctor Lawrence to Bolivia.

Back in Cochabamba, I met up with Doctor Lawrence for a briefing before our visit to Silvia. I told him we wanted him to approach this subject forensically to the best of his ability.

'I want you to examine this statue like you would a corpse at a crime scene,' I said.

He was totally up for the challenge. We liked Lawrence. He had a curious mind and we could see he truly wanted to figure out how things worked.

We arrived at Silvia's, Doctor Lawrence armed with his full kit of scalpels and lights. Silvia gave him permission to take samples from anywhere he liked. Ron filmed the doctor's entire examination of the statue.

'It does look like blood. It looks authentic,' he said.

It was not actively bleeding at the time, but Lawrence found an area below the ear where the dark red substance felt slightly moist.

'It has the characteristic sheen on the surface, a very shiny look to it . . . It looks exactly like dried blood looks at a crime scene.'

He completed his examination but, unfortunately, he could not illuminate the mystery of our statue any further.

'For myself, on a very personal level,' he said, 'I would prefer this to be a trick.'

But if there was a trick to it, he couldn't find it.

He wasn't staying in Bolivia long, but while we had him, we thought we might as well use his experience of examining severely traumatised bodies by showing him some pictures of the wounds that had appeared on Katya's head during the stigmata. Without telling him the backstory, Ron asked if he could tell how such wounds might have been made.

'Those injuries look very much like what I've seen in cases where someone is thrown out of a car in an accident and their face is brushing up against thorny vegetation,' Lawrence said.

He certainly didn't think they were caused by someone surreptitiously cutting themselves. We then talked about *Signs From God* and you could see him, as an atheist, grappling with the implications of what this might all mean if it were true. I don't think he changed his spiritual orientation but the impressive thing about Doctor Lawrence was that he was just plain interested.

One thing Doctor Lawrence did point out to us was that there were parts of the samples from the statue that he could not identify under the microscope. He suggested we find more experts to run down what these things were.

Ron sent one sample to a lab which came back and told us that the substance was of 'non-human origin'. He sent more samples off to a number of different laboratories and waited. Eventually a scientist at Westmead Hospital in Sydney's west, Doctor John Walker, came back with an answer.

It was a plant. But because of its structure, the doctor added, 'My feeling is that this is of a "spine" which grows in a fairly dry sort of area.'

Ron asked him if he meant a 'thorn'.

'Yes,' Doctor Walker replied. 'The plant that comes to mind is a date palm which has really vicious thorns around the base, or hawthorn. If they stick into you, they break off, but the tip stays in the skin.'

We could not help but think of the awful, mocking

coronation of Jesus at His crucifixion. It is not known what species the crown of thorns was made from. Though a relic purported to be it is housed in Notre Dame Cathedral, Paris.

The slides from Silvia's statue had also revealed other cells that puzzled Doctor Lawrence. Ron found a pathologist with expertise in the identification of human cells, Doctor Richard Haskell, from his hometown of Gosford.

Doctor Haskell recognised what the other cells were: non-keratinised stratified squamous epithelial cells – the cells that form the outer-most layer of skin in moist areas of the body, like inside the mouth.

'It is abnormal to find such cells in blood,' Doctor Haskell said. 'The mixture seems to indicate that the flesh had been wounded and bled. But the injury would not have been caused by a sharp knife or scalpel. A sharp cutting object would sever the flesh and create bleeding but not introduce a multiplicity of epithelial cells stripped of their outer keratin layer. No, the injury was caused by a blow or blows from a crude, blunt object which fractured and traumatised the tissue.'

We revealed the source of the sample, and Ron asked if it was possible that someone could put such tissue on a statue.

'To do so, the person would have had to use something like a serrated saw to cut their skin in tiny pieces and then mix it with blood and then put it on the statue.'

It seemed a little hard to imagine Silvia doing that.

Twenty-two

Opening my Heart

Looking back, one of the questions that really confuses me is why I took so long to not so much convert as *revert* back to the faith of my childhood. *Signs From God* seemed to inspire a lot of people to embrace Catholicism – but not me.

By this time, I'd witnessed so much, it was hard to explain why I hadn't crossed the line and said, 'I believe in God and He's clearly there. I believe in Him and I want to follow Him. I want to tell people about Him.'

For some reason, I held back.

I was still the professional reporter, or trying to be, telling these stories but not buying into them myself. There was some blocking mechanism, a cognitive dissonance, that stopped me from following my instincts and drawing the logical conclusions from the stuff that I was seeing with my own eyes.

Around the year 2000, Ron brought Katya and Father Renzo out to Australia. I had just completed a renovation of an old hotel that I'd bought in North Sydney – The Union. I was very proud of it; it was my first such endeavour.

I invited them to come and have dinner at the hotel's flash

new restaurant. I wanted it to be perfect. I had some highly qualified chefs, and I spoke to them about the importance of my guests for that night, and how everything had to be spot on.

As we waited for our meals, I was talking and talking about my wonderful renovation, as if no-one had ever done such a thing before. I'd redone the whole hotel, which included offices upstairs for my production company, Trans Media.

Just as the meals began to arrive, Father Renzo broke into my monologue with his heavy Spanish accent.

'Michael, so your offices are up there?'

'Yes, Padre. Yes, they are.'

'Have you had them blessed?'

I had to stop from laughing because I hadn't even had *myself* blessed since I was in my early teens. As if I'd have my offices blessed. I didn't even know you could do such a thing. Especially above a pub.

'No, Padre,' I said, respectfully.

'Would you like to?' he asked.

'Thank you, Padre, that would be nice.'

I said it out of politeness more than anything, thinking that we might come back over the next few days and do whatever ceremony was required to bless an office. Waft a bit of smoke around, sprinkle a bit of water.

But Father Renzo got up immediately and headed for the stairs.

Oh, no, the food's just been served. It's perfect. It's ready and we're off to bless the offices?

But I dutifully got up and followed the priest. Katya followed me.

As we ascended to the office area upstairs, all clean and modern, I explained how the renovation had been so well planned and architect-designed. But Father Renzo seemed not so interested. He walked over to the smallest space there, the nook where we made our tea and coffee. I didn't follow.

'Michael, what is this room?' he called out to me.

I thought he was losing it. It seemed self-evident that he was in a tearoom. But I walked over.

'Father, this is just where you make tea and coffee.'

He took me by the shoulder and guided me into this tiny room and he made the sign of the cross and I knew instinctively — I don't know how — that he was starting confession. The concept of confession was frightening to me. I had a backlog of 40 years' worth of sins. But suddenly I'm in the firing line, with a priest asking me to confess them.

My first thought was to wheedle my way out.

Father, no, no, no — I'm not ready, I've got to prepare for this. I've got to think about it.

But I didn't. I found myself submitting to the process.

It was strange because Father Renzo came from South America, so his perspective was different to ours. For example, when he was prompting me for sins that I'd forgotten, he asked, 'Did you kill anybody?' I don't think any priest in Australia would ask that without a specific reason. I wanted to smile but I couldn't because I was too uptight.

He completed the confession, and at the end of it I'm thinking, *But I haven't told him everything. How can I, after more than 40 years of living the high life?*

And then he said, 'For these sins and those you have forgotten, you are forgiven.'

I felt a heaviness come off my shoulders. Thinking back, I can see that it was probably the prospect of confession that had been my subconscious roadblock back to faith. But now I walked outside, weightless, and I saw Katya in the foyer, praying and crying. She came to me, and she hugged me, continuing to cry. By now, I was crying too.

Katya then reached into her dress and pulled out a holy card, which depicted Jesus holding the prodigal son. I was stunned because I was replicating that story of the prodigal son. I was coming back after a long absence. I could not explain how Katya knew this was going to happen, how she came to have the perfect holy card for what I had experienced.

That holy card has now been around the world with me maybe 20 times and it still looks new. There is something very special about that card. I later asked Father Renzo where Katya got it. And he just pointed upwards . . . to God.

Even then I could sense that the reason I felt this weightlessness was that I had known for several years that there was a God because of the work I was doing, but I hadn't had the courage to say so, to stand up and stand for it. But suddenly it was true. It was easy to say, easy to believe. I was saved.

Part Seven

Continuing the Work

Twenty-three

The Host

Once I had accepted my return to faith, my interest in looking into claims of God's intervention only deepened. It was no longer a case of a journalist chasing down a story; it was a personal choice for me to continue on my spiritual journey. And, hopefully, to find some proof for the rest of world along the way.

In January 2002, Ron and I took another trip to a small city in South Korea, Naju. There was a woman there named Julia Kim who had gathered a large following based on a string of claimed mystical events. Communion hosts had turned to flesh on her tongue. Hosts had fallen from above around her. She was said to have undergone the stigmata. Statues had bled, pictures had bled, and we were told she had received messages.

We didn't know very much more about her, except that she had a very strong following and she seemed to be quite orthodox in her Catholic beliefs. We found ourselves driving down a very narrow road between a canal and some houses trying to locate her place. When we did, we could see that it had once been quite a reasonable-sized residence, but she had been excising parts of it to convert to a big hall where her followers could gather on Saturdays, traditionally the Virgin Mary's day.

We were met by Julia and her close supporters and we walked around and saw the pictures and statues that had bled, and it was interesting, but it wasn't the evidence we needed to be able to say that we were looking at something authentic here.

I was impressed by the sheer number of people she had involved. There were swarms of them, mostly in the big hall. When we finally sat down for a meeting, we were taken to her bedroom. That was pretty much all that was left of her home. That was where things got interesting. The room was tiny, and she had a lot of her supporters crammed in with us. We were sitting on her bed, but there were others on chairs and on the floor. Meanwhile, somebody brought some snacks and drinks in. Julia picked up a piece of food using a small, two-pronged cocktail fork and offered it to somebody when, out of nowhere, she and her guest were thrown violently to the floor. It certainly didn't look like they'd done it themselves. It gave us a fright and was quite dramatic.

Julia took it in her stride as if it happened all the time. Her supporters told us that, yes, indeed, the Devil attacked her often. She picked up this little cocktail fork and it was bent completely. That was not evidence of anything, since you could bend that flimsy little fork quite easily, however, it too was quite dramatic. While we were sitting there, starting to talk about this, she was thrown off her chair again, and once again it seemed authentic: she just flew sideways off her chair onto the floor. As before, it didn't seem to bother her. She took her place back on the chair and we continued talking.

And then – I didn't see it at first, but most of the people in the room did – two communion hosts came down from up above. When I say communion hosts, I had no idea whether they were consecrated or not, but they were the standard type of communion wafer, and they appeared to come straight down on a trajectory from a point in the middle of the ceiling. We searched the ceiling and there was no place apparent from which such an object could be launched and the way they came down together on a vertical trajectory made us think they had not been tossed.

This was not hard evidence, but it gave us more to think about.

The following morning, Julia took us up the back of her property where the land went up a fairly steep hill on which she'd built the Stations of the Cross. There are normally fourteen steps in the Stations of the Cross, which represent the stages Jesus went through in the lead-up to His crucifixion, from Him being condemned to death up to His body being placed in the tomb. Julia had fifteen steps and some theological argument for why that should be so. We followed her up the slope in the heavy snow as she went from station to station, praying. She was kneeling on about the sixth station when she suddenly lifted off the ground. I'm only talking about inches, but she left the ground and was thrown some metres down the slope. One of the men in her group moved in quickly to stop her from sliding further down because the snow had become very icy. I was wearing normal city shoes and I could hardly stand up myself. I had to be supported. This happened two or three more times and by the time we got back to the house, we noticed that she had a significant bruise on her face.

It was frustrating for us because we left without any hard evidence. We'd seen some interesting things, but Ron and I simply did not know whether we thought Julia Kim was an authentic mystic or not.

I suppose the strongest memory I have is the determination and enthusiasm of her supporters. They certainly believed in her.

Twenty-four
Jesus' Command

Ron and I were by now spending more time with Katya. It was a privilege to be in her presence: we had absolute faith in her and what she was saying. We'd be sitting around, and Jesus could join the conversation, speaking through Katya, as if He were just another one of your friends. No matter how often it happened, I never quite got used to it. One of the most surprising aspects of Jesus joining us just like another one of the guys was how simple and practical He could be.

In March 2000, we were in Israel preparing for a three-day visit by Pope John Paul II – the second ever papal visit to the holy land after Pope Paul VI spent a single day there in 1964. We had arrived in Jerusalem with inadequate preparation and no accommodation booked, presuming we would simply find something when we got there. But the Pope's visit was turning out to be a much bigger thing than we'd anticipated. No matter how hard we tried we could not get accommodation. We needed a Plan B. We were sitting around with maps and guides, exhausting all the possibilities in the ancient city.

After a lot of time wasted, Jesus made His presence known to Katya.

'Why do you have to stay in Jerusalem?' He asked her. 'Just move a little further out of town. You'll get accommodation and catch the bus in every day.'

All of us kind of looked at each other.

Why didn't we think of that?

On another occasion, in May 2002, Ron and I were in Miami with Katya, Father Renzo and Ricardo Castanon, sitting around talking about some of the documentaries Ron had made on the faith, when Ricardo told us that he, too, had made a documentary. It was about the Eucharist.

'I'd like you to see it,' Ricardo said.

He put a DVD into the machine and translated it from the Spanish as it played. He had all the information in there, but it was crammed. It was fact after fact after fact. There was no pause for reflection, no music, hundreds of pictures running too fast together. It was a solid effort for someone who'd never made a documentary, but I was a little uncomfortable because I knew I'd be asked my thoughts and I didn't want to say, *That's not going to get to air, Ricardo. No-one's going to play that.*

Then Katya piped up. 'Jesus has asked that Mike give to Ricardo your opinion.'

This was even more embarrassing. Ricardo was a new friend. I didn't want to criticise his work, so I gave some mealy-mouthed answer, like, 'It certainly has all the information in there. That's what the Eucharist is all about as I understand it.'

Katya interrupted, 'No, Jesus just said tell us what you *really* think. What is your *professional* opinion?'

The word 'really' embarrassed me more than the instruction

itself. I felt skewered. If this was Jesus speaking, I could hardly continue to mince my words. I had to be direct and honest, yet I still didn't want to offend Ricardo.

'Well, in its present form it's . . .' I searched for my words carefully, '. . . it's not suitable for television, but it does have all the information there, it just needs more space, time to think, time to reflect on the important pieces, maybe a little bit of music, and so on . . . Ricardo, it is difficult to make what you have done work with television.'

Katya interrupted again. 'Jesus says He agrees with Mike.'

Ron couldn't help but smile at that, easing the tension somewhat.

Katya continued. 'He says, "Mike, I want you to make an English version and make it so that it can reach the greater part of all humanity."'

Ron has since told me that his recollection of this conversation was that Jesus also said He wanted it to be finished by August. It was already May.

No pressure!

We had to come up with something that reflected how important this ceremony was to the Church and, we felt, to Jesus. There was no shying away from it. We connected it back to Katya's earlier message that, through the miracle of the Buenos Aires host, Jesus wanted to bring dignity back to His altar.

From a personal point of view, I had to face facts. I'd seen Katya's stigmata with my own eyes. It was real. I believed her, so I had to believe what she was saying. I had to believe the huge importance that she was telling me Jesus placed on this ceremony with its wafer of unleavened bread and its sip of wine. I felt we'd been privy to a very special occurrence with the host in Buenos Aires. It was all pointing us in one direction – to use that information to bolster the argument that this is for real.

But it was not as straightforward as you might think.

Since Jesus' last year on earth, there's been a tension among His followers about whether Jesus was speaking metaphorically or literally when He told the disciples to eat of His flesh and drink of His blood. Protestants tend to believe it is more of a metaphor, while the Catholic Church continues to say it is literal – that when that wafer goes on the tongue, you are consuming the real presence of your saviour. They call it transubstantiation, whereby the substances might continue to look like bread and wine, but they have in fact been transformed into the body and blood of Christ.

Among Catholics in general, however, the belief in the 'real presence' of Jesus in the Eucharist is fading. There was a study in 2010 that revealed that half of all American Catholics weren't even aware of the Church's teachings on the subject. And the surveys generally say that about 60 per cent of Catholics do not believe in the real presence. That it is just a metaphor. In Australia, a survey showed that only 27 per cent of final year students at Catholic universities believed in the real presence.

Here was a core teaching of the Church being, at best, not understood and, at worst, completely rejected.

By the time of our meeting in Miami in 2002, even though our investigations of the Buenos Aires host were far from complete, we'd seen enough to convince us that there was substance to this transubstantiation.

Here's what the Gospels say about what happened at the Last Supper:

> Mark 14:22: While they were eating, He took some bread, and after a blessing He broke it, and gave it to them, and said, 'Take it; this is My body.'

> Luke 22:19: And when He had taken some bread and given thanks, He broke it and gave it to them, saying, 'This is My body which is given for you; do this in remembrance of Me.'
>
> John 6:56: 'He who eats My flesh and drinks My blood abides in Me, and I in him.'

Ron and I felt an enormous responsibility weighing on us to convey a very traditional view of the Eucharist, and by August, with Ron riding shotgun, we'd put a good little film together called *The Eucharist: In Communion with Me*.

Of all the shows I've made, it is perhaps the one that has most fulfilled me.

Towards the beginning of the film, I pose the question:

> But what of that mystifying teaching that the communion host, having been consecrated in the Mass, is now, truly, flesh of Christ? And that the wine in the miracle of the Eucharist is now truly the blood of Christ? In fact, the teaching of the Church goes even further, that in the Eucharist is the living presence of Jesus Christ. Just as real and just as alive as He was on Earth more than 2000 years ago. Yes, Jesus Christ truly there. Flesh, blood, soul and divinity. Can that really be the truth and, if it is the truth, why do we not see Catholics eager to approach the altar in greater numbers at every opportunity to receive communion and be embraced by Jesus, son of God? Let us look for the answers through Jesus.

We put the death of Jesus in the context of a sacrifice by God. Remembering the ancient traditions of sacrificing an animal to your God then eating it. After all, Jesus ate the sacrificed lamb of the Passover at the Last Supper. Again, me speaking on the film:

> So, when Jesus gave us the gift of the Eucharist at the Last Supper, it was consistent with that tradition. The great difference being that He is the victim being sacrificed and He invites us to participate in His great sacrifice, by eating His flesh and drinking His blood. That was a concept that was to trouble many from the days of Jesus right through to today and Jesus knew that it would. Well before the Last Supper, at the town of Capernaum, Jesus made the almost unbelievable promise that He would give His own flesh and blood to be the food for our souls. He prepared His audience well. On the day before, He performed the miracle of the loaves and fishes. Five loaves and two fish fed thousands . . . On the night before, He walked on water. They should have been ready to believe in Him.
>
> Even then, Jesus knew that doubts about the reality of the sacramental gift of His body and blood would persist in the centuries to come. And so it would be that Jesus would intervene, miraculously, to endorse the truth of this sacrament.

The documentary then followed us going to Lanciano in Italy where we showed the remarkably preserved state of the communion host that has been on public display for 1200 years since it had transformed in front of a doubting monk. For its endurance alone, science had no answer. We showed our interview with Professor Linoli who found that the Lanciano host was made up of heart tissue.

We went to Orvieto to show a procession that's been held every year for 500 years to mark another host that started to bleed in front of another doubting priest who wiped up the blood with a linen cloth. It was the incident that prompted the then Pope to launch the feast of Corpus Christi, the body and blood of Christ. In Orvieto, that same linen cloth is still paraded through the streets, the blood stains still clearly visible.

We then went back to Buenos Aires, and the communion host there, to show that this was an ongoing thing. That going right back to Capernaum, Jesus knew that His gift would be a test of faith for many, and that we'd need a bit of proof to help us along.

Perhaps our most important theme was encapsulated by the question: 'Do we not profane His divinity when we see the host as a mere symbol of Christ's body and not the reality of His presence?'

We wanted to get across the message that the Last Supper wasn't just to give of His flesh to the apostles, but for them to pass down this miracle through the bishops and priests who would follow.

As I said in the doco, 'When you think about it, this is an awesome power. As the priest raises this small piece of bread in consecration, he makes it become our saviour, the creator of the universe, the one in whom lies all human hope and merits salvation. The one who sustains all with His infinite power.'

It was an emphatic statement of the traditional view of the Eucharist. We had a lot of support from traditionalists in the Church, but some more 'progressive' types found it too old-fashioned. Given what I'd seen, however, I felt duty-bound to present it this way. You can't be a witness to such things and then hide it. I know that a lot of journalists could not, would not, do it like this because they'd fear the ridicule.

But my life was at a point where such things no longer mattered. What did matter was my lifelong commitment to telling the truth as I saw it.

Twenty-five

Seeing Clearly

The film came together well and quite easily, everything seemed to go right for us. It was launched in Sydney by the Sydney University Catholic Society. They made a big event of it and showed it a number of times to large audiences around Sydney, so that was gratifying. It was well received by the people who accepted the traditional views, but ultimately the confirmation that something powerful was happening came when we took it on the road.

Over the course of the next year, Ron and I travelled the country showing the film and giving talks. When we showed it in the South Australian capital, Adelaide, in November 2003, there were about 700 people in the room. It seemed to go over well. Then Ron and I participated in a Q&A session following the screening. The emcee asked that the questions be kept short.

'There are a lot of people here who we'll want to get to, so please don't make statements, just questions, so Ron and Mike can answer them all for you.'

One of the first to get to the microphone was an old man who tapped his way forward with a white stick.

When it was his turn, he said to the emcee, 'I know you said questions only, but can I make a short statement?'

I might have groaned a little on the inside. *Here we go.* But we indicated for him to go ahead out of deference to his senior status.

'My name is Harold O'Shea,' he said. 'I'm 84 years old and basically you could say I am blind. But tonight I came along to hear Mike Willesee and when the film started . . . I saw . . . perfectly . . . clearly the whole film. I watched it right through and then lost it on the credits.'

He had everyone's attention now. We were stunned into silence.

Harold continued. 'When it started, I said, "Lord, please let me see this film because I know it's going to be special." And He did. I saw the lovely little girl receiving communion on her tongue and her bright pure eyes as she looked up at the priest and said "Amen" and I saw everything in focus . . . just perfectly right to the end.'

'And now?' I asked.

'Now it's back to the way it was before. It's . . .'

Overcome, he couldn't go on and sat back down.

Later, I was signing autographs onto tapes of the show. There was a long line, and one woman couldn't wait. She edged in.

'The same thing happened to my friend too,' she said, looking nervous.

'The same what?' I asked.

'My friend Pauline sitting next to me. She saw the film too.'

'That's nice. Did she enjoy it?'

'Very much,' the woman replied.

'That's great,' I said blandly, but I could sense she was getting frustrated by me.

'No, I mean she *saw* it. She's blind too,' the woman said.

'Legally blind. She didn't want to say anything herself because she didn't want people thinking she was jumping on the bandwagon because you're here and everything.'

Then the woman turned and walked off.

'Come back!' I said.

But she'd disappeared into the crowd.

A couple of weeks later, Ron and I returned to Adelaide to interview Harold O'Shea and perhaps the mystery woman, Pauline, if we could find her.

We went to Harold's home and he told us that he had macular degeneration and was only capable of seeing vague outlines of shapes. He showed us some sort of optical instrument that he usually used to help him read text and how it enlarged individual letters up to the size of a page to allow him to see them. He'd taken this device to the screening thinking it might help him see the film, but it was playing up, so he put it down in disgust, thinking that he'd wasted his time in attending at all.

But then he'd looked up and been more than a little surprised that he could see the screen. Not only could he see the film, but he had firm opinions on what he thought were the best shots.

'My vision went again after the film,' he explained. 'I was blind again. I don't know if it was better that I had my sight restored or that I saw that film.'

Ron and I spent some time with Harold, and we were very impressed by him. And as we observed the layout of his house and his monocular instrument he used to help him with his little remaining sight, there was not the slightest doubt in our minds that we were dealing with a genuine person with an authentic experience and one that was beyond our understanding.

What impressed us most was that he continually went back to talking about the film, rather than his own personal experience. He bought four copies to give to friends and we later heard that he'd been able to bring several members of his family back to the Church with the film and his incredible story.

We hadn't been able to get an address for the mystery woman, Pauline, but not long before we were due at the airport, we managed to locate her. Her name was Pauline Grzeszkowiak. She had just returned home with some girlfriends after a day out shopping when we arrived. I had to wonder how blind she really was.

She told us she had only 5 per cent vision, caused by macular degeneration.

'It's peripheral only, so if I turn to my side to look at you, I can see a blurred outline of where you are.'

'Can you see me?' I asked

'No, I know you are there, but I can't see your face. It's like I can see an outline of a tree, very indistinctly, but I cannot see any leaves.'

Ron, who was filming, zoomed in on her face and you could see her eyes had that straight-ahead look of a blind person.

'So why did you come to the hall that night if you knew you wouldn't be able to watch the film?' I asked.

'I didn't know there would be a film. My friends told me that you were giving a talk and so I came along with them.'

She went on to describe visual aspects of the film, congratulating Ron and me on our efforts.

'Where is Ron?' she asked.

'That's Ron, there. He's filming you,' I said.

He was standing no more than two metres away, silently filming. She turned side on and tried to squeeze out that little bit of vision from her periphery.

'Can you explain why it happened?' I asked.

Continuing the Work

'I think the grace of God came over me for some reason.'

The priest who had been our master of ceremonies that night pointed out that since the medical evidence was that these people shouldn't have been able to see the film, and since they did see it, that it was a powerful proclamation of the truth.

'If a blind person was able to see the film, then you can take it as a sign from God that He wants the film seen.'

This was an interesting point to make, considering that it was exactly what Katya had told us that Jesus was saying at that meeting 18 months earlier. His message that day been that He wanted us to go ahead and make a documentary for all humanity.

Well, Ron and I had made one – and we went on to have it translated into Spanish and Polish too. We went to Poland to launch it there and it was received very well. One of the bishops said that everyone should have it by their bed, like the Bible, because it was that important. And Catholic television in the United States played it every year for a number of years on the feast of Corpus Christi.

We felt we had at least put it out there for a large chunk of humanity.

Twenty-six

Sacred Heart

Making the documentary caused a bit of a hiatus in Ron's and my other investigations, but they were never far from our minds. The failure to obtain a genetic profile from the blood samples still appeared to be an enormous stumbling block. Upon preliminary testing, we'd consistently been told that it was human blood or tissue and that there should be no problem getting a DNA profile from it. But when it got sent off for DNA screening, it always seemed to go wrong and they'd say they couldn't obtain a profile.

When Doctor Lawrence had the slide up on screen, he'd pointed to a blood cell.

'Look at the size of that white cell,' he'd said. 'You'll get all the DNA you want out of that.'

We sent some of that sample off for more DNA testing, but again, we were told that no human profile could be obtained. The samples were degraded.

Ron was off doing his own research and he twigged that there was something not quite right in this explanation. The way he explained it to me was that when a sample becomes 'degraded', it means that the individual cells in the sample have broken down and the material within the cell has leaked out.

Yet we'd seen the cells in Doctor Lawrence's microscope, and they were not degraded at all. Rather, Lawrence had specifically told us that they were in pristine condition. This realisation changed our whole focus: the problem was not the degradation of the sample. There had to be another reason why we were not getting the code.

Ron doesn't give in easily, so he sat at his computer all night looking for new options. DNA technology was improving rapidly during this time. He found a woman from a German university who claimed that she could get results from very small samples. She agreed to see us, so within a day we were on a plane flying to Germany.

It was freezing cold upon our arrival in Göttingen and as we were straight off the plane from Australia, we were dressed only in light jackets. We had left in such a hurry that we hadn't put any thought into packing. We ran from the train to the taxi, then from the taxi to the university building to stop from freezing.

We introduced ourselves to the young scientist, Susanne Hummel, and she introduced an older man as her professor.

'I thought it was wise to have my professor with me,' she said, looking nervous.

She cross-examined us about the source of the sample, but we didn't want to tell her because we knew from experience that it didn't go over well. And that any results obtained would be affected by bias if we told the purpose of our quest.

'I'm not going to talk any further unless you tell me,' Hummel said.

She dug her heels in. We felt we had no choice but to tell

her about the general direction of our research, without getting too specific. But before we got very far, the professor cut in.

'We won't be examining this sample,' he said from behind Hummel.

'Why not?' I asked.

'Because I know what's in there,' he said, motioning towards the package, which was thickly padded and taped up and sitting on the desk in front of us.

'Well, you're a scientist . . . How do you know?'

'I know, and I'm not going to do it. *We* are not going to do it.'

Ron got talking to Hummel, who added, 'Our university doesn't do this sort of thing. We're atheistic. It's part of where we stand.'

She explained that what they found might embarrass the university and they risked having programs shut down.

We couldn't budge them.

We ran back out into the freezing sleet and returned to the airport to fly all the way back to Sydney.

I'm not the type of reporter to give up easily. There's always a way to get the story. But even I was starting to think this one was too tough. I was ready to admit defeat.

Ron, however, was not to be deterred.

He kept digging and came across a bloke called Tom Loy from the University of Queensland. Loy was both an anthropologist and an expert in cellular biology – he was also the only real-life scientist mentioned in Michael Crichton's novel *Jurassic Park*, owing to his groundbreaking work on identifying blood – and what species it came from – on ancient tools and weapons. He was at the time working on analysing DNA preserved in blood that he'd located on the tools and clothing of the 3000-year-old 'Iceman', Ötzi, whose frozen body was found in the Alps between Italy and Austria.

When we met with Loy, he said he was working on a way of deciphering the code of damaged DNA. We funded him to do some research in that direction and he worked on this procedure for some time. We were waiting for him to get to the point where he could say he'd worked it all out for us, but unfortunately, he died suddenly at his home, aged 63.

Upon Loy's death, we came to realise there was little point continuing to try to reconstruct the genetic code of the sample cells. The pathology showed that the cells were intact; that there was no degradation of the material. Quite simply, they should have given up their genetics. The reason that they had not, we were forced to hypothesise, was because they didn't have a genetic code. At least not as far as contemporary science had come to understand such things.

And how could it understand when everyone and every creature previously studied had come about from the combination of male and female DNA.

We had to face up to the teachings: Jesus had not arisen from such a union. He was not the son of man.

One of our major conundrums was that we had three scientists – Doctor Lawrence, plus two Australian professors – telling us that the Buenos Aires communion host was skin tissue, but we had the anatomist and pathologist from Italy, Professor Linoli, saying it *might* be heart tissue. Linoli was outnumbered, sure, but this was too important a point to leave hanging.

At this time, the internet was really starting to come into its own and Ron wasn't afraid to get on it and start teaching himself about heart tissue. He told me he must've gone through thousands of images and dozens of textbooks on the identification of human cell tissue.

He got to the stage where he could look at something on

the screen and say, 'That's textbook epidermis. That's textbook heart tissue.'

But that still didn't explain how Professor Linoli could think our sample might be heart tissue while the others thought it was skin. Ron eventually stumbled onto a university website where he saw an image of a slide that looked a lot like our slide of matter from the Buenos Aires host. The caption said it was heart tissue that had been affected by constriction of the blood supply. It even said that, under such circumstances, the tissue could be confused with epidermis.

Eureka!

Suddenly, he could see the problem. We'd been looking for the textbook version of an apple, but our apple had been hit by a sledgehammer and looked more like an omelette. Ron realised he needed to find someone who knew hearts and who knew what trauma did to them. And after many more sleepless nights on the computer, he called me one morning in 2004.

'I think we might have found the right person to go to. He's a heart specialist, a cardiologist who's also a former County Medical Examiner. He's been a forensic pathologist since 1969. He's written books. He's even got a disease named after him. He's retired, but he's still working, and he lives just outside of New York City in a place called Poughkeepsie.'

Ron and I had never heard of this town 100 kilometres up the Hudson River north of Manhattan. However, we made an appointment and got straight on another plane.

Given our past disappointments, we were not optimistic. Once we got to New York's Grand Central station, we realised we couldn't even pronounce the name of our destination – it turned out to be something like 'po*kip*see'. We managed to find and board the right train and it was a spectacular journey along the banks of the mighty Hudson River. Then we missed our stop. It just seemed that everything was going wrong.

When we eventually got to the house of Doctor Frederick Zugibe, we found a man who was visually exactly what we wanted. If you'd called Central Casting and said, 'Give us an eccentric professor', you'd be very happy if they produced this guy for you. He had curly white hair and a white goatee.

Ron had an unobtrusive little video camera that was actually quite a high-quality piece of equipment. He pulled it out of his bag.

'Is it okay if I film Mike with this?' he asked Doctor Zugibe, who happily agreed.

But for all that, once the doctor got us inside his office, he wasn't very welcoming.

'I haven't got much time for you,' he said. 'Tell me what it's about.'

As usual, Ron had tried to tell him as little as possible when they'd been liaising over the internet. He'd written that he was a lawyer working on a case and he needed to identify the tissue in some slides. Ron had sent pictures of the slides and Doctor Zugibe had written back saying that it looked like heart tissue, but that he needed to take a look in person.

And that was as far as it went until we turned up on his doorstep.

It was totally normal practice for any forensic pathologist to want to know the history of a specimen before examining it, just as a doctor takes the history of a patient before doing any tests. But we felt we couldn't give him that.

'We can't tell you because it could compromise your findings. It's a very sensitive matter,' I said.

'No, that's no good for me,' Zugibe said. 'I've been a County Medical Examiner for more than 30 years. The police call me.

I go to the scene of a crime, the scene of an accident, they say, "It's a white male, six foot, 200 pounds, suspected gunshot wounds." So I know a lot before I get there, and you're telling me nothing?'

We continued to argue our point with this wise older man.

'It's important for us that you have a clear view of this,' I said. 'We'll tell you everything after you've had a look at it.'

He finally conceded to our point that if he knew what it was about, the impartiality of his findings would be compromised.

We took the sample out of its thick protective packaging and he took a cautious look. He placed one of the slides under a microscope and his reaction was almost spontaneous. Thanks to Ron's video, I can quote him verbatim.

'I am an expert of the heart,' he said. 'The heart is my business. This is flesh. This flesh is heart muscle tissue, myocardium from the left ventricle wall, not far from a valvular area.'

I was struck by how specific he was being for a man having his first look through a microscope.

'It is the muscle that gives the heart its beat and the body its life . . . This heart muscle is inflamed. It has lost its striations. It is infiltrated with white blood cells. White blood cells are not normally found in heart tissue. These cells are produced by the body and they escape from blood and infiltrate the tissue to address trauma or injury. The heart of the person from which this tissue has come has been injured and suffered trauma.'

I could feel a rising sense of excitement.

Zugibe said it could be the heart of someone who'd suffered a heart attack.

'The person had to have lived a period of time after this. For, oh, at least a few days after this. Now, there's other things that can cause this kind of item that resembles a heart attack. An automobile accident where they get chest crushing that causes damage to the heart. You get it from a person being beat up across the chest. You get coronary injuries in people who have had CPR incorrectly.'

He went to his files and pulled out a recent case of a man who'd been whipped to death. It looked the same to me.

As to the age of our sample, Zugibe thought that given the degeneration he saw, the muscle structure and the type of white blood cells present, the trauma had occurred two or three days before the slide was prepared.

'What was recognisable was the complex process of the human immune response in action at a defined point in a defined biological process.'

He knew exactly what had happened.

'The myocardial condition was not caused by the death of a person. The slide showed no evidence of death. This sample was alive at the time it was collected.'

I let that one sink in for a moment.

A lot has been made of my famous pause while interviewing people. Perhaps too much has been made of it. Often, it's just me trying to figure out where to go next, knowing that the wrong question could let an evasive interviewee off the hook. Best to say nothing than to say the wrong thing.

But this one had me gobsmacked – alive at the time it was collected!

'And how long would the white blood cells remain vital if they were in human tissue that was placed in water?' I eventually asked.

'They would dissolve within minutes and no longer exist,' Zugibe said with great confidence. 'Now, what's the history?' he demanded in that assertive, New York way.

I told Doctor Zugibe that this sample had been kept in ordinary tap water for a month, then distilled water for three years.

'That's impossible,' he said. 'White blood cells cannot exist outside the body because they are fed *by* it. White blood cells normally dissolve within minutes to an hour of being taken from the body. Furthermore, it would be impossible for the white blood cells to be present in the sample if the sample had been kept in water. The morphology of the tissue showed good fixation. I would only expect to find such a good state of preservation if this tissue had been placed in a preservative like formalin.'

What he was saying about white blood cells dissolving in a matter of hours reflected almost exactly what Doctor Robert Lawrence had told us four years earlier. So that was no surprise to us, but I had a surprise for him.

'And what would you say,' I continued, 'if I told you that the source of this specimen was a piece of wheaten bread, a communion host?'

Ron's camera recorded the scientist's eyes widening as he processed the information and composed a considered response.

'How or why a communion host could change its character and become living human flesh and blood is outside the ability of science to answer.'

Thankfully, Zugibe was happy to put all this in a written report for us. He wrote that the inflammatory cells were consistent with a recent blockage of the heart (a heart attack) or a strong strike across the chest.

He was absolutely clear in what he observed. There was just no doubt in his mind. He saw it so clearly and so quickly. Ron and I both had a feeling at the time that we had found the answer — that Zugibe had cracked the code.

When we walked out of there, one of us said, 'It's going to be hard to appreciate the magnitude of what we just heard, what we've just uncovered.'

We were both working through the ramifications with a strong sense that all the effort we'd made in getting to this point had been rewarded. We knew this was a very important discovery, but that we still had to work hard to understand the implications of it.

Meanwhile, we had to get the train back to Manhattan ahead of our flight back to Australia the next day. We were getting to know a lot of airports. But at least we now had a certain clarity. Professor Linoli had already told us he thought it could be heart tissue, and Zugibe's background and his firmness on the point were even more convincing.

Nevertheless, we owed it to Doctor Robert Lawrence (who thought the material was epidermis) to give him a chance to rebut the new information. And that's precisely what we did.

When we presented Lawrence with Doctor Zugibe's findings, he softened. He's a very open-minded and intelligent guy.

'Yes, I can see why somebody would say this is not just heart muscle, but traumatised heart muscle,' he said.

Later, at a meeting with us in 2008, he said that he had reconsidered his opinion and that he had in fact been wrong. The tissue, he said, was *definitely* inflamed heart muscle.

Twenty-seven

The Blood of Christ

Back in 1995, on the day that Doctor Ricardo Castanon took the first blood sample from Silvia Arevalo's statue in Cochabamba, Katya had received a message from Jesus.

'I want the blood that is wiped from my image to be given to the Church authorities and for it to be compared with the blood of my Shroud. It is time for the lies to be buried and for the truth to be revealed.'

In one of his filmed interviews with Katya, Ron had asked Katya what she thought Jesus meant by this.

'I understand that when the blood from the statue is compared with the blood on the Shroud of Turin,' she said, 'they will find that the blood is from the same person and that this will assist in the authentication of the Shroud of Turin as the true burial cloth of Jesus Christ.'

'Do you realise what the consequences for you will be if the blood does not match?' he asked her.

'I trust my Lord,' she smiled.

Katya was putting her reputation on the line for Silvia's bleeding statue. If we could test the blood from it and compare it to blood from the Shroud of Turin and they were different, Katya would be exposed as a fraud. There is no room for mistakes when you're channelling the Lord. But if Katya was right, and the blood from the statue matched the blood on the Shroud, the implications would be mind-blowing.

Our next challenge, of course, was how to get access to the Shroud: you just can't march in and say you want to take a blood sample from the Shroud of Turin! As perhaps the most venerated – and controversial – relic in all of Christendom, it is, understandably, well shielded from an army of 'investigators' who'd like to get their hands on it.

A lot of people are under the impression that carbon dating in 1988 exposed the Shroud of Turin as a medieval forgery. What they don't realise is that those researchers took a corner piece of the Shroud that showed signs of being a patch. All they proved was that somebody tried to fix it up sometime between 1260AD and 1390AD, by which time, if we are to believe it truly is the burial cloth of Christ, it would have already been exceedingly old, and so probably in need of a few repairs.

We made contact with the people who were the custodians of the Shroud but knew that in order to be taken seriously we had to go wider and get a substantial body of work together to convince them of our capabilities. There were a lot of relics to choose from.

In Spain, in Monasterio del Escorial, for example, there's an enormous collection of relics donated by King Phillip II in the 1500s. He was quite a forward thinker who embraced modern western ideas, yet he collected these relics, including 10 human bodies, 144 heads, 306 arms and legs, as well as claimed hairs of Christ and bits of the crucifix. Among all that, there was one item in the collection that particularly interested us.

During the Reformation, some Protestant Dutch soldiers had broken into a church and began to destroy the hosts that were in the tabernacle. One of the soldiers put his boot into one of the hosts and that host began to bleed. King Phillip II eventually got hold of this host because he saw it as an important sign from God that the claim of the Catholic Church about the transubstantiation was real.

We hoped that we might be able to get access to that host and be able to test the blood. We met with the custodians and they took us deep into the vaults below the monastery, which is part of an enormous complex of a cathedral, royal palace and library. They told us the story and showed us the relic and it was an inspirational moment to be shown it, but they also explained that the building was World Heritage Listed, which included all of its contents. Therefore, we couldn't do anything with the relic unless they got agreement from the World Heritage List bureaucracy and that was highly unlikely to happen. We pushed back, but soon realised it was going to be too hard a mission to be able to do that test.

Next, we tried to get access to the Lanciano host that Professor Linoli had studied and declared to be heart tissue. We thought that the Buenos Aires case gave us a lot of credibility in making this request. Ricardo Castanon had, after all, been personally asked to investigate that one by the then auxiliary bishop, Jorge Bergoglio, whose star had risen swiftly. He is better known now as Pope Francis.

But even being able to wave that name around didn't seem to help us and we weren't able to successfully pursue it.

While the Shroud of Turin was still our ultimate goal, there was one other relic which we saw as being just as important – the Sudarium of Oviedo.

Here's what we know about the Sudarium from John 20: 6–7, describing when Simon Peter ran into Jesus' tomb after Mary Magdalene had alerted him that the stone gate had been rolled away: 'He saw the linen wrappings lying there, and the cloth that had been on Jesus' head, not lying with the linen wrappings but rolled up in a place by itself.'

Those 'linen wrappings' are the Shroud, the 'cloth that had been on Jesus' head' is the Sudarium – *sudarium* means sweat cloth in Latin. The story goes that before Christ was taken down from the cross, they placed a cloth over His head to absorb the blood that was streaming from His injuries. The cloth was kept because of the Jewish tradition that blood is sacred, and so it was put in the tomb with the body. It stands to reason that a group of disciples would gather these last connections to the man they had venerated who had disappeared, especially a head cloth.

The next mention of it is by Antoninus of Piacenza who wrote in 570AD that the Sudarium was being cared for in a cave near the Monastery of St Mark close to Jerusalem. It was taken to Alexandria from Palestine ahead of a Persian invasion in 614AD and then on to Spain soon after as the Persians pushed into Egypt.

In 718AD, it was taken to northern Spain and hidden in a cave as the Moors advanced up the Iberian Peninsula, until, in 840AD, a chapel was built to house it in Oviedo, Spain.

While the Shroud of Turin contains an image said to be that of Christ imprinted on it by having been draped over His body, the Sudarium, on the other hand, is more like a rag that was used to soak up the blood and thus had no obvious images on it.

In 1998, civil engineer Guillermo Moreno, forensic pathologist Professor Jose-Delfin Blanco, and a specialist in the study of the Shroud of Turin, Professor Jorge Manuel Almenar, published a study comparing the blood stains on the Sudarium to the markings on the Shroud.

Their findings were remarkable.

First, the blood stains were human, type AB. They also found that the dirty, creased and torn cloth with several burnt fragments appeared to be a funeral cloth that had been wrapped around the head of a man with a beard, a moustache and long hair tied into a ponytail. The man's mouth was closed, and his nose was pushed to the right by the pressure of the cloth. At the back of his head, there were a series of wounds caused by a sharp object while the man was still alive. Blood covered the man's head, including his hair. And about an hour after those wounds were inflicted, the cloth was placed on top of them. He was not breathing by then.

They also found that the man had suffered a pulmonary oedema (fluid on the lungs) as he died, causing bloody liquid to come from the nose and mouth. The cloth was placed over his head from the back and went around the left side of the head to the right cheek, where it was folded on itself, 'like an accordion'.

'Once the man had died, the corpse stayed in a vertical position for around one hour, and the right arm was raised, with the head bent 70 degrees forward and 20 degrees to the right.'

The authors concluded that the only position that explained it all was crucifixion.

They found that the body was then placed on the ground on its right side, with the arms in the same position. The forehead was placed on a hard surface. The body was moved some more and someone 'tried to stem the flow of liquid from the nose and mouth, pressing strongly against them' as evidenced by fingerprints on the cloth.

Continuing the Work

'The cloth was then straightened out and wrapped all around the head, like a hood, held on again by sharp objects . . . Finally, on reaching the destination, the body was placed face up and for unknown reasons, the cloth was taken off the head. Possibly myrrh and aloes were then sprinkled over the cloth.'

According to John 19:38–39, after the crucifixion:

> Joseph of Arimathea, who was a disciple of Jesus, though a secret one because of his fear of the Jews, asked Pilate to let him take away the body of Jesus. Pilate gave him permission; so he came and removed His body.
>
> Nicodemus . . . also came, bringing a mixture of myrrh and aloes, weighing about a hundred pounds. They took the body of Jesus and wrapped it with the spices in linen cloths, according to the burial custom of the Jews.

The geometric testing of the Sudarium and the Shroud (which also contained Type AB blood) showed that the injuries and blood marks matched, reinforcing the view that the two relics came from the same body.

The Moreno–Blanco–Almenar team concluded: 'Information both for and against both cloths has been coldly and scientifically evaluated. Our conclusion from this is that in both cases it seems much more possible that the cloths are genuine than the opposite.'

Ron and I got in to see it, which was an enormous privilege in itself. In history, kings have been denied access to this relic. They took us down into the vault of the cathedral and there were seven locks on the door, each requiring a separate key that was held by a different person, all of whom had to be present together to gain access. It was an incredible honour to be allowed in. We were able to get that far because they valued the work we'd been doing up to this time. But again, that was as far as we got.

There were two others that we were also working on, though. One was in Bruges, Belgium. According to legend, after the crucifixion, Joseph of Arimathea wiped blood from the body of Christ and preserved the piece of cloth in a vial. The relic remained in the holy land until the Second Crusade, when the King of Jerusalem, Baldwin III, apparently gave it to his brother-in-law, the Count of Flanders, who brought it back to Bruges in April of 1150AD, where he put it in a chapel he had built on Burg Square.

However, recent historical research found that it was more likely that the relic found its way to Bruges after the Christian city of Constantinople was sacked by the army of the Count of Flanders, Baldwin IX, during the Fourth Crusade in 1204AD.

Whatever its origin, the phial played a huge role in the religious life of the city until it slipped into a certain obscurity in more modern times.

Scientific tests on the phial revealed that it was a Byzantine perfume bottle made of rock crystal, dating back only to the 11th or 12th century. But the age of the bottle was not evidence of the age of what was inside it. It has never been opened since it arrived in Bruges. The Byzantine perfume bottle is encased in a glass-fronted gold cylinder, on which the date of 3 May 1388 is engraved. Which of course only tells us when the cylinder was made.

It was a potentially significant item that had none of the notoriety of the Shroud or even the Sudarium. There's a chance it is a fake, but from our point of view it is, potentially, a brilliant reference point. If it did happen to match our samples from Buenos Aires, and if it did happen to match future samples to be taken from the Sudarium or the Shroud, again, the implications would be mind-blowing.

Ron had a stockpile of these sorts of things that we could explore. A passage from John 19:23–24 tells us:

> Then the soldiers, when they had crucified Jesus, took His garments and divided them into four parts, to every soldier a part, and the coat. Now the coat was without seam, woven whole from the top down. Therefore, they said among themselves, let us not tear it, but cast lots for it, whose it will become.

According to legend, that garment ended up with the mother of Constantine the Great in the 4th century and had then found its way to the great emperor Charlemagne who gave it to his daughter, Theocrate, Abbess of Argenteuil, in what is now a suburb of Paris.

In 1793, the parish priest, fearing that his 'Holy Tunic of Argenteuil' would be desecrated in the French Revolution, chopped it into pieces and farmed those pieces out to various noble families. Only four pieces came back to Argenteuil. But some of those do appear to be bloodstained. This is another trail of blood that could lead, ultimately, to the Shroud.

We can't guarantee we will ever get access to these relics or be able to test them in the way we want to, especially in our lifetimes. But the fact remains that these are items which, if proven to be linked via blood samples, would be the biggest story in history. We can only do what we can to pursue our research and with the technology improving all the time, if we can complete the tests, well, then perhaps that information will link back to some of our samples.

*

While Ron and I kept up our investigation and attempts to access and test the relics, we also continued to research those who had claimed to have experienced interventions from God.

In 2005, we went to Poland to launch the Eucharistic documentary in Polish. While there, we took a particular interest in the story of Sister Faustina Kowalska. She was a Polish nun who died in 1938 at the age of 35 claiming to have had a string of conversations with Jesus. Among her many instructions from Him was for her to paint a portrait of Him and to devote the first Sunday after Easter to His Divine Mercy. Belief in her grew strong after her predictions of a great war came true, but the Church, fearing a cult of personality, banned her teachings in the 1950s.

A young archbishop named Karol Wojtyla was given the job of studying her original writings which resulted in the ban being lifted in 1978. When Wojtyla became Pope John Paul II, he stood before the world and said he believed that Jesus did speak to Sister Faustina and that He said important things about humanity to her. John Paul II canonised Sister Faustina in April 2000 and inaugurated the feast day Divine Mercy Sunday on her designated date.

That was interesting to me because it is highly unusual for a Pope and the Church to publicly endorse this kind of claim. Yet Pope John Paul II didn't hold back from proclaiming the reality of what he believed had happened. He himself was a mystic. After his death, it was revealed that he too had recorded conversations with Jesus in his diary. Prudently, he kept them to himself, but it is clear he had a strong connection to such directly spiritual phenomena.

So there definitely existed people of substance in these modern times who genuinely believed that the creator did speak through people at different points in history. And it's interesting that some of the writings of Sister Faustina reflect what Katya says she's been told.

For example, Faustina said she was told by Jesus, 'I want my Eucharist honoured because my heart is in the Eucharist.'

Now, that's a funny thing to say: 'my heart is in the Eucharist'.

Yet here we were having found heart tissue in the Eucharist from Buenos Aires. Sister Faustina became of great interest to us and we interviewed people in Poland about her life.

That year, we also went to Lanciano again and presented an Italian version of our documentary to the custodians of the 8th century Eucharistic phenomenon there. We thought it couldn't hurt to try to get our foot in the door for getting access to the ancient relic down the track.

Twenty-eight

Convincing Australia

In 2012, I felt like I needed a new challenge, so I went back to television, joining Channel 7's *Sunday Night* current affairs show.

I loved being back on the road doing the rounds of political interviews, celebrities and criminals, but one assignment that really stood out for me was the death-row interviews of the two Bali Nine ringleaders, Myuran Sukumaran and Andrew Chan. I got to spend time with both men in jail over four days and witnessed the way they worked incessantly running courses, helping other inmates and, in the case of Chan, leading Bible studies. They'd both converted while in prison. I know that a lot of convicted criminals 'find God' as a facade to help garner sympathy. But I could see the way they kept at it, even when the cameras were off them and they thought I wasn't watching. Chan said that he'd asked God to set him free and that God spoke to him. 'Andrew, I have set you free, from the inside out. I have given you life.'

It was one of the saddest stories I'd done. I was in Sydney when Myuran and Andrew were executed in 2015 and it nearly broke me. They may have started off as criminals, but they were proof of Christ's power to redeem.

While I loved the work I was doing, I kept my eyes on the biggest story of all – the real presence of Jesus Christ. The executive producer at *Sunday Night* knew about the work I'd been doing all these years and was interested in maybe having me do something for the show, but it was still a big call for a secular outfit like that to go off chasing miracles.

I knew better than anyone that you had to be prepared to endure some ridicule if you were going down that road. But, as I reminded them, the last time I'd followed this route on mainstream television, 28 million Americans tuned in to watch. Numbers like that can help the most thin-skinned executive producer endure a bit of scorn! But it wasn't enough to get me the go-ahead.

The catalyst came when I was renegotiating my contract, holding out for more money, and they dangled a carrot they knew I couldn't resist.

'We'll let you do that blood of Christ story you've been going on about.'

I took the carrot and signed.

We began in mid-2015. Ron came in and authorised the producers to use the footage he'd filmed over the years, not to mention the considerable file of scientific test results and the expertise he'd accumulated. His only stipulation was that they not use it in a derogatory manner. He didn't push for any greater controls because he knew he had me on the inside to help guide things through.

There was old footage of me interviewing people like Doctor Robert Lawrence in 2001 and Doctor Frederick Zugibe in 2004, so there was a risk that I might look a bit old in any new material by comparison, but fortunately I'd just finished a story where chef Pete Evans had fed me and guided me through a 10-week paleo challenge. I was looking the youngest and feeling the fittest I'd been in years. I was walking without pain, which, having had a bad hip, was something I hadn't experienced for years. I was sure the viewers would hardly notice the leaps in time.

Ron and I had a stock of samples that could be tested, but Ron made the point that we had to be very careful with where we chose to get them examined. He argued with the story producer, Alex Garipoli, and me that it would be a waste to send them to the Victorian Institute of Forensic Medicine, in Melbourne, because every test done previously had shown there was no human genetic code in them.

'When you do these tests, you can't make any distinction between what is touch DNA and what is DNA from the cell itself,' Ron said. 'So, as time goes on, the chance of contamination is greater and greater. All the lab in Melbourne is going to do is get our sample, stick it in the melting pot, DNA will come out and they'll measure it. They can't make any distinction between who's handled it, who's breathed on it and what the substance is.'

'These are reputable people,' I said. 'They know what they're doing.'

And besides, the show had to be seen to be getting our own tests done rather than relying on old material gathered by Ron and me.

But Ron was ready for us.

'I've been doing research into all of this and if you can take out a single cell from your sample that's inside the material – in our case a blood cell – and get a DNA reading from that one cell, then it must give you a more accurate result. Until you can do that type of testing, we're going to risk this problem of contamination.'

Continuing the Work

Our challenge was that we were dealing with this phenomenon of there appearing to be no DNA in cells which we had tested umpteen times. If there was touch DNA contaminating the sample, that was going to be the only stuff that would show up in the results. And since more time had passed since the original samples were taken, there was a greater likelihood of that contamination being a problem.

But within the constraints of the show, and in the absence of anywhere better to send them, it was decided that we'd just send the samples off to Melbourne for testing.

In the meantime, we had a program to make. And a good budget to make it. We spent more than a month travelling Latin America, gathering some beautiful shots and some great interviews. The idea was floated that maybe this could be a two-hour special. After all, if you can pinpoint the blood of Christ, that's a pretty big story.

We went back to Cochabamba where Silvia's daughter, Kim Arevalo, now a doctor, told us what it was like growing up in the shadow of their miracle statue. She said it had probably cried and bled 800 to 1000 times over the past 20 years. We took the statue back to the same scanning laboratory we'd taken it to all those years ago for the latest in three-dimensional scanning. Every crack and hole would be clear to see. I asked the head of the laboratory what he could see.

'This is the second time we do this scanning of this image. The first time was 20 years ago. And the results are the same. We don't see any trick here.'

'So there's nothing inside the statue that could produce any liquid on the outside?'

'No, there is nothing.'

In Argentina, we re-interviewed the photographer Marcelo Antonini, and he cried as he told us how he had been a non-believer when he'd been called in to take the pictures of the Buenos Aires bleeding host in August 1996. But it had changed his life forever.

We travelled to Tixtla in Mexico to investigate a host that had bled in 2006. It had fallen from the hands of a woman who was in a wheelchair. The *padre* went to pick it up and saw that it was stained with 'blood'.

Our old friend Doctor Ricardo Castanon had been called in to investigate this claim and he submitted it to all the most rigorous tests he knew. Those tests found that it was human blood, type AB – the same blood type as identified on the Lanciano host and the Shroud of Turin. Furthermore, while the outer layer was old and crusty when it was tested four years after it first appeared, the layers underneath revealed fresh blood! And 'immunohistochemical studies reveal that the tissue found corresponds to the muscle of the heart (myocardium)', the official report to the Church stated.

But Tixtla, about 200 kilometres south of Mexico City, was no easy place to travel. Just to get to the church I needed to be accompanied by a ute full of men with rifles in case we drew the attention of the local drug cartel. The *padre* very kindly allowed us to take a sample from his precious host that had become known as the 'Miracle of Mexico'. He had to take it out from behind bulletproof glass.

We also got wind of a host that had started to bleed in a tiny dusty town called Campoalegre in central Colombia. Just before Easter in 2006, a nun was carrying a large consecrated host to the church in a metal container. When she opened it, she was stunned. The host appeared to be bleeding.

'It was like fresh blood,' she told me. 'It was something inexplicable.'

I asked her what she thought.

'We had our doubts. How did it happen? Who did this?'

Unlike the other such events that had happened across Latin America, the Church in this case told them not to talk about it. The local bishop was fiercely sceptical. We took a sample. And we were lucky we got there when we did. Soon after we left, the bishop turned up and took the host and buried it in the garden. He was apparently afraid of bringing controversy to the Church.

The local priest was astonished at what his bishop did.

'Jesus said, "This is my body. This is my blood." The Church has always assumed this is true and they have always defended it. So this is extraordinary,' he said to us.

I called the bishop seeking an explanation, but he didn't respond. Nobody in the nearby town had even heard of the bleeding host, which was just 30 kilometres away.

I did a piece to camera telling the *Sunday Night* audience how I'd had the blood of our older samples tested again and again in laboratories around the world, and each time the result was the same. The blood was human, but each lab failed to find a DNA profile. I spoke of my 20-year quest to find the truth behind such things and you can hear me almost boasting about how much DNA technology had advanced in the two decades I'd been on the story. So advanced, I said, that a single human cell can be tested and its origin revealed.

We re-interviewed Doctor Robert Lawrence, whose beard had greyed a lot since the old footage we showed of him early in the episode. He was older but certainly just as open-minded as he'd always been.

'I don't believe in God,' he said. 'But then again it would be exciting and wonderful if this turned out to prove the existence of God. I think that would be great. I would love to be proved wrong.'

The story was coming along really well. We had all we needed. We just had to wait for the test results to come back.

But when they did, they were not what we'd expected.

In early November 2015, the Victorian laboratory got back to us saying that they had found female DNA in the sample from Silvia's statue.

Ron then sent Silvia's genetic profile to the lab.

That same day, Doctor Dadna Hartman replied saying that Silvia's profile matched that found on the sample from her statue. To everyone else on the case, it was a huge dampener. It made it look like fraud.

For Ron though, it was precisely what he'd warned of. This was just as likely to be 'touch' DNA from Silvia's handling of her statue as it was to be the DNA of the substance oozing out of the statue. He was adamant that finding Silvia's DNA on the statue proved nothing. And I had to agree. She owned it. She kissed it and touched it. It would be more surprising if her DNA didn't show up on it.

Eventually, Alex agreed that we should do the single-cell analysis. The people at the Victorian Institute of Forensic Medicine were helpful. They steered us towards a lab in Bologna, Italy – Silicon Biosystems – that had the ability to pick up a single cell and analyse its DNA. In this way, they could ensure they were testing a blood cell from the statue and not, say, a flake of Silvia's skin. They could, effectively, cut that blood cell open and analyse the DNA inside it, decreasing the likelihood of picking up touch DNA.

Doctor Francesca Fontana ran some preliminary tests on our samples. They passed the presumptive test for the presence of blood. And the quality looked good.

'For a strong sample like this, if it was human DNA, I should have no problem getting a result,' Doctor Fontana said.

Continuing the Work

What did they find?

Well, no surprise to Ron and me, 'no human genetic profile was found,' Fontana's report said. 'We cannot explain why no results were obtained.'

It wasn't because of a lack of material to work with.

'We were really surprised to find so much data from the samples,' Doctor Fontana told me. All the samples yielded human white blood cells. Human tissue cells were also identified. Yet they were unable to get any DNA.

The team from Silicone Biosystems saw this failure to get a result as, well, a failure. The producers at Channel 7 saw it as a failure. It took the wind out of their sails. When you're hoping to find the DNA of Jesus but get nothing, it can be somewhat deflating.

Ron and I, however, saw the no-result as confirmation of all that we'd been seeing over the last 20-odd years. That there was a phenomenon at work that was beyond current understanding. This more precise technique also contradicted the findings of the Victorian lab's approach which had picked up Silvia's DNA on the sample.

We felt like we needed more time. When Doctor Fontana had said she got 'so much data from the samples', what did that mean? Surely that data would show something if we could just find the right person to interpret it for us. We set off to find an expert who could tell us. Ron encountered the usual problems when he'd ask the most prominent people in the field to take a look. They'd google his name and see it associated with 'woo-woo stuff' and flat out refuse to even look at what we had. It seemed we had hit an all too familiar roadblock.

As 2016 rolled on, I had a couple of interviews lined up in Los Angeles with the actor Mel Gibson and my old mate Paul Hogan . . . and that's when my life entered a new phase.

Part Eight

A New Phase

Twenty-nine

Unfinished Business

After interviewing Mel Gibson, I am in pain, chewing through painkillers, knocking back the booze. The crew cancels the Hogan interview and takes me to hospital. I am drunk, but my team senses there is something else the matter. The hospital runs a bunch of tests and sends me back to my hotel.

'The guy's just had too much to drink.'

My voice has gone strange, the pain in the side of my face won't go away. Back in Australia, my doctor sends me to the dentist who pulls some teeth, does a root canal, but fails to ease the pain. An ear, nose and throat specialist sticks cameras up my nose and down my throat . . . then puts his hand gently on my shoulder.

I know I'm a goner before he says a word.

It is throat cancer and, after a barrage of more tests, they tell me I have six to twelve months.

Well, that's going to focus your mind on what's important, isn't it?

Aside from tending to my family and tending to my relationship with God, this story is it for me.

But Channel 7 wants more and is holding the story until Easter 2017. *Sunday Night* has been taken over by a new executive producer who I doubt sees stories such as the one I'm working on as part of his long-term plans for the program. I want to be there to steer this story through, and I just want to work. That isn't to be, however, and my final days of paid employment are spent coming in to voice a few bits and pieces for the story which we are by now calling *The Blood of Christ*.

I have now had the most indescribable experience of seeing someone in heaven. I know that is a big statement and one which will be questioned by many. But my belief in the authenticity of this experience is unshakeable.

Ron's wife, Gabrielle, died on 17 January 2014. She was a very good friend of mine. In fact, she was a very good friend of everyone she met. She was just that kind of person. She travelled with us on many of our adventures – millions of miles around the globe – while we put together *Signs From God* and our other investigations. I was a regular visitor to her home and I knew her well. She was a woman of extreme charity. She constantly went out of her way to help anyone who was in need – the poor, the hungry, the sick, the dying, the old person down the street who just needed help with their shopping. Gabrielle was just always there, an inspiration for those of us who would like to live a better life.

It has never crossed my mind that anybody would appear to me from heaven. It's not the sort of thing that happens to me. But I'm at Mass in Sydney's St Mary's Cathedral on the first Sunday of December 2016 when, suddenly, Gabrielle is there. It is an innocuous image of her that I see but, oh, so powerful:

A New Phase

her full face, her hair and a hint of the top of her shoulders. She does not look at me and I get the impression that she is oblivious to the fact that I can see her. She appears to be listening to someone, maybe diagonally across the table from her, but close.

I am stunned by how beautiful she is. She was a beautiful young woman when I first met her, but she was in her sixties when she died and her looks, as you'd expect, had changed. But there is not the slightest doubt in my mind that this is my friend, Gabrielle. She appears as if she is in her late twenties and her beauty is beyond what I had encountered in life; smiling quietly with a look of contentment and relaxation.

When Ron later asks me to describe what I saw, I have trouble finding the words because the ones that come to mind, like 'beautiful', 'relaxed', and 'serene', don't seem sufficient. They are too common and overused. Then the right word comes to me in a jolt: 'heavenly'.

So there she is, almost like I am watching a wall-sized television barely two metres away, until she disappears as quickly as she had materialised, leaving me in a pleasant state of shock.

Looking at it now, I can wonder if this was a message related to my fate. Was she telling me I'll be joining her soon? Or that everything's going to be okay? That I'll be cured! But I don't ask myself those questions at the time. They seem to simply not matter. I just feel great comfort . . . and joy.

Six weeks later, Ron calls me with some news.

'Somebody else has just had an almost identical experience with Gabrielle as you had,' he says.

Ron explains that he has a friend from Melbourne (who I'll call 'Burt' because he's asked not to be named). Burt and his wife, Anne, were regular visitors to the New South Wales Central Coast and whenever they were around, they would join Ron and Gabrielle Tesoriero in their weekly prayer group.

When Burt rang Ron to tell him about the apparition, Ron asked Burt, who is also a lawyer, to write it down.

Burt wrote: 'On the evening of Saturday 14 January 2017, I went to bed about 11.30 pm. A few hours later, 2.30 am, while still asleep, a young and very beautiful woman appeared to me. I thought she was aged in her twenties. I could only see her from the shoulders upwards. Her face was beautiful. She was happy, peaceful and heavenly. There was a certain luminosity about her face that was hard to describe.

'She looked directly at me but said nothing. That vision took up the whole scene. I only knew Gabrielle when she was about 60 years of age. I did not know what she looked like in her twenties but somehow, I knew it was definitely Gabrielle.

'Immediately after the vision, I woke up. The whole thing was very real to me. When I woke, I could recall every detail and immediately woke my wife, Anne, and told her what had happened.'

Ron had not told Burt about my vision beforehand so there was no question of prompting. When he did tell Burt my story, Burt revealed that he had been diagnosed with thyroid cancer and he believed that could be related to Gabrielle's appearance. That her appearance was 'a great consolation' to him.

I have never met Burt, nor had I even heard of him before this. I don't need the coincidence of his story to confirm my certainty about my vision of Gabrielle, but it is nevertheless very pleasing and uplifting news. Burt also later tells Ron that after the intercession of Gabrielle, his tumour is no longer visible to his medical team.

Two things have stayed strongly with me since that news about Burt. One is his comment about Gabrielle's appearance being of 'great consolation' to him. The words I had used in my

A New Phase

report to Ron were that her appearance was a 'great comfort'. Different words but precisely the same sentiment.

And second, he'd used 'heavenly', the very word that I had struggled so hard to find.

I have managed to get into a trial for the new immunotherapy drug Keytruda and by Christmas all my tumours have shrunk to the point where the doctors can hardly see them anymore. I've lived such a charmed life, I keep expecting them to tell me I'm cured, that it's some kind of miracle. I can't understand why they don't tell me I'm good to go. Surely if the cancer is almost gone, I've almost beaten it. But they refrain from such magical thinking. I'm still terminal.

However, they at least allow that I will outlive the original prognosis of six to twelve months.

Channel 7 is going to run *The Blood of Christ* at Easter in 2017, but we have it complete and in the can a couple of months ahead of that. Ron gets to see a draft version and isn't happy. He rings me and voices his many concerns and after hearing him out, I've got to say, I agree with him. The bulk of the 31 minutes deals with material I have already outlined, but in the last few minutes it all goes wrong.

As the show nears its conclusion, we present it, incorrectly, as though we had gone to the Italian lab first and found no DNA and only then came to get it tested in Australia.

'The clearest interpretation of any of the cases came from a tiny fragment of the "Miracle of Mexico",' I say in the voiceover. 'We brought it back to Australia to be tested at the Victorian Institute of Forensic Medicine. And like the other samples, it was identified as human, but in this case, there was more information.'

My voiceover reveals that we have found the DNA of a woman in one of our samples, implying that it's the one from Tixtla in Mexico.

'So it's not the result of a divine event,' I say. 'It even suggests there may have been a well-orchestrated fraud.'

I turn to the camera.

'So whose blood is it? Without testing every woman who's had access to the *host* [my emphasis], it's impossible to tell.'

We switch back to voiceover.

'This Mexican event is now commonly described as a miracle and the Church has declared it a divine sign, but it seems to have failed the scientific test, but try telling that to the believers.'

I'm then riding in a cab, talking to the camera.

'I began this investigation as a sceptic and the results from the Mexico case tend to make some of those doubts a little stronger, but the inability of 20 years of scientific research seeking clear answers to the other so-called miracles underlines the depth of this mystery – which means to me this case is not closed.'

Those are my last words as a journalist on television. And they are a dog's breakfast. As are all the show's conclusions. I clearly wasn't thinking straight when I read the script. For a start, the sample that had been thrown into doubt was not the Miracle of Mexico sample. The female DNA had, of course, been found on Silvia's statue. And the DNA was identified as belonging to Silvia. We'd had the test results showing it was Silvia's DNA since November 2015.

But just like Ron had warned before we even started the story, there was a high probability that this was touch DNA. What we don't mention is that DNA of the producer, Alex Garipoli, was also detected in the sample from the Buenos

A New Phase

Aires communion host – and he never even touched it with his bare hands. He must have breathed on it at some point. That just shows how easily these things can be contaminated.

Ron had trusted his material to *Sunday Night* because I was there to keep an eye on things. He needs me now to go in and fix this story up. But things have changed at *Sunday Night*. The new executive producer is no friend of this story. He just wants to get it off his plate with as little embarrassment to his reputation as possible.

I am also sick, undergoing chemo and immunotherapy. I have no power in an organisational sense and no strength in a physical sense. I am in no position to fight; to say, 'The conclusions you've come to are based on scientific tests that are not foolproof.'

Or even just to say, 'You've got it wrong.'

Ron has more leverage than me since he owns the footage that Channel 7 wants to use and hasn't signed it over to them yet, but he is also stuck in a bind. He doesn't want to embarrass me by taking out an injunction on the show.

He writes an angry-lawyer letter.

He says that even if you forget the mistakes the show has made, what the story needs is a couple of lines saying that reputable forensic pathologists say that the Buenos Aires sample is made up of human heart tissue – that bread has turned to flesh! – yet after more than 20 years of testing, it has never yielded any nuclear DNA profile. That the same is true of the Miracle of Mexico. That the program gave no weight to all the science that has preceded it. That the risk of touch DNA having polluted Silvia's statue sample means you can't draw any conclusions from that. That *Sunday Night* did the more precise single-cell testing on Silvia's statue sample *after* the more primitive Australian test – and did not find her DNA (nor that of the producer) in it. And that even if Silvia is a fraud, it does not detract from the mysteries of the other cases.

There is a token attempt to address Ron's concerns with a rushed end-piece statement by the show's presenter, Melissa Doyle, and the story airs.

We are gutted.

That story is my last hurrah after 50 years of television. It should be my most important. My best. But it is a missed opportunity. If you pull it up on YouTube, you can hear my voice sounding different in different parts, and me looking different as I go from apparent robust good health to throat-cancer sufferer. And you'll see those errors we put to air.

Ron keeps saying to me, 'Just imagine if the truth of this story was properly revealed, Mike. Imagine the effect it would have.'

And I can imagine that.

I do imagine that.

I finish my *Memoirs* and while it is being edited, I get started on this manuscript, which will become the focus of my final days. In August 2017, Ron and I travel to Bolivia to interview Katya again for this book.

One thing Katya says to me towards the end is that, 'Not one leaf moves without God knowing.'

It will stick in my mind.

Back home, I am sitting on my balcony, privileged to be overlooking the ocean with a strong wind blowing, white caps blasting off the peaks. I'm going through my notes from our latest meeting with Katya and a gust of wind picks up a loose

A New Phase

sheet of paper and takes it on a wild joy flight. I don't know what is on that particular page, so I don't know the importance of what I've just lost to the wind. But watching the piece of paper looping and fluttering at high speed up to the top of the five-storey building then down to the ground and whipping through the garden in a tumultuous eddy, I accept that with my poor health I have no chance of going downstairs and catching this leaf on the loose.

I say a small prayer.

'Jesus, if I need that piece of paper, you can get it and I can't.'

About an hour after the paper had flown away, I glance down at the garden and notice a sheet of paper about the same size as mine. It is lying there with what appears to be a heavy stick lying on it.

My immediate reaction is, 'Well, that can't happen. A piece of paper can't fly into a garden and insert itself under an object. My curiosity gets the better of me and I go down and it *is* my piece of paper.

And it *is* important.

Katya tells us many things in our meeting, but it is when I ask her about her relationship with Pope John Paul II that she confides an extraordinary story.

'In 1998, I went to a conference in Rome which a number of my group had been invited to. My spiritual adviser, Father Renzo Sessolo, was invited also but was delayed on his arrival because he was travelling with our Archbishop, René Fernandez,' Katya tells us.

'When we finished dinner one night, we gathered so we could get ready to pray, but Our Lord said to me, "Get ready because you will meet the Pope tonight." I did not know when or how that would happen. And the only people I told were my two closest friends there. Then I fixed my hair and held one of my recent notebooks that I had been using to take dictation from the Lord. I had it next to my chest.'

Katya continues: 'Then the Lord said to me, "Lie down." I lay down on the bed and began to pray and I told my friends, who were sharing the room with me, not to do anything, just to pray. I then added, "Even if I go flying out the window like Superman."'

I have to interrupt her at this point because it sounds like she's taking a bit of poetic licence. 'Did you actually say, "Even if I fly out the window?"' I ask.

'Yes.'

'Was that a joke?'

'No . . . I did not know how I was going to see the Pope. I just knew that I had to lie down on the bed. I did not know if it would be a dream or if the Holy Father was in fact going to fly in. I did not know what bilocation (the experience of a person being in two places at the one time) was.'

She resumes her story.

'I went to sleep and when I woke up, I was in a different place. I saw the Holy Father, John Paul II, from behind. Without turning around, he said, "Is that you, Katya? I was waiting for you, Katya." He had his rosary in hand and was saying the rosary and then he turned around and I fell to my knees and I started crying. He held out his hand and I kissed his hand. I asked him to forgive my sins because I had judged him badly because I thought a pope had to be like Pope Pius XII. I told him everything and then he said, "Don't worry." And then he saw that I was bare-footed, and he kicked some slippers over to me.

A New Phase

'"You forgot your slippers . . . I was waiting for you. You should have come with a priest." He then appeared to be thinking and he touched his head as if in thought. He said, "Oh, he is flying in with the Bishop." I knew he was flying in with Bishop Fernandez. Then I gave him the book and I asked him to give us his blessings for all my family and my life. I also wanted a blessing for the work I was now starting. He gave his blessing. And he gave me a wink after the blessing. The Pope also said the Church was going through a very difficult time and we needed to pray a lot and not to be afraid. He then left and I opened my eyes to find I was back in my bedroom with my friends.

'They were crying and praying, scared, very afraid. Shocked. They asked what had happened. I then said to them, "Well, what happened to you?" And my friend said, "One moment your body was elevated, your body was on top of the bed, but elevated, and there was a space between your body and the bed. And when you returned your body dropped back fully onto the bed."'

Katya says she then asked her friends not to tell anyone until she had a chance to speak with Father Renzo. They then went to sleep. Father Renzo arrived with Archbishop Fernandez the next day.

I interview Katya's friends about the incident and ask them about the bed during the time that Katya was undergoing this experience. They both agree that the indentation around Katya's body disappeared. She was lying on it, but it was as though she had no weight. Her body did not push down into the mattress.

After that, there was a second occasion of a bilocation with Pope John Paul II. Over the years, Katya had told Ron and I on numerous occasions of the problems she was having with a particular archbishop. She felt persecuted because he wouldn't allow her to publish the messages she was getting from Jesus.

'One night when we were in Merida, Mexico, I was sleeping in my room and I felt the presence of someone. I turned around and found myself in front of a tall window with light coming in; in that light, I saw the figure of a person in front of me. He said, "Be calm, it is me. I want to tell you that I sent a person to talk about you with Archbishop Berlie. Don't be afraid. I will always look after you." My visitor, who just appeared in my room, was Pope John Paul II.

'Days later, David Lago, a very close friend of ours, had a meeting with Archbishop Berlie and started talking about me and told Berlie that the Pope supports me. Berlie asked, "Why do you say that?" David responded, "Because the Pope is looking after her." Berlie questioned why he would say such a thing. "Has not a person from Rome, from the Pope, come to talk to you about Katya?" David asked. Berlie confirmed that a person from the Vatican had come to see him and had mentioned Katya in passing.'

To me, this is very important because the question of bilocation is one which is difficult to support with evidence even though we know it is accepted within the Church under certain circumstances. We know that one of the Pope's right-hand men, Archbishop Francesco Monterisi, a Secretary of the College of Cardinals and Secretary of the Congregation of Bishops of the Roman Curio, did visit the archbishop and that permission was then given for Katya to spread the messages.

Katya's story continued.

'The Bishop had sent the books to Rome so they could be studied by this order of priests in their own university. They studied my books and Monseigneur Berlie said, "If the books have a contradiction or an error, I'm going to prohibit them . . . The University of the Legionaries sent a document to Monseigneur Berlie saying they had studied the books and they had found no errors.'

Katya's happiness with her ability to publish and distribute the material she had received from Jesus was short-lived, however. When Pope John Paul II died in 2005, Archbishop Berlie promptly reimposed his prohibition of Katya's work. It was clear that the protection that John Paul II promised Katya was indeed there in his lifetime but was not respected by Berlie upon his death.

During this visit with Katya, I am still struggling with my health and I excuse myself to go and have a nap. While I sleep, Ron pulls up the *Sunday Night* story and shows it to Katya. He tells me about it afterwards.

'I said to her, "Why wasn't there a positive response from the findings in Italy? What went wrong?" She said that Jesus said this to her: "Those white blood cells did not have their normal shape and the reason is that when the body undergoes trauma and suffering the white blood cells change their shape to go in and address the trauma and suffering. And that that trauma and suffering is what I suffered in my Passion."'

To my knowledge, Katya knows nothing about the physiology of white blood cells, but here she is, somehow having an insight into the testing results; that hidden in those results is evidence of His trauma and suffering during His Passion.

After that, Ron dives into researching white blood cells and confirms that, yes, they do change their shape when there is trauma. They move out of where they are and change their shape to infiltrate the traumatised area to deal with the problem.

How does Katya know that?

Anyway, her take-home message for Ron is to keep testing. To keep going.

It gets Ron into surfing a new wave of scientific thinking where they are finding that trauma can affect the genes. And that there is certain mitochondrial information that's released from organs affected by trauma that goes into the bloodstream and gets picked up in mitochondrial DNA tests.

And it's in the mitochondria that the answers to this question we've been chasing all these years will probably be found. Remember, mitochondrial DNA does not come down through both parents. You get all of it from your mother. We've spent all this time chasing the nuclear DNA – the type that comes from both parents – of a person who didn't have a human father.

If we follow the mitochondrial DNA, perhaps we can find the link between the Shroud and the bleeding hosts and the bleeding statue to fulfil Jesus' instruction to Katya – to bring dignity back to His altar.

Ron is onto it, but I'm nearing the end. Those tumours that disappeared in the early months of my illness, well, they've come back.

In 2018, Ron goes and gets Silvia's blood tested by the latest mitochondrial sequencing equipment at the Australian Genome Research Facility. He brings me the results at my Bondi flat in December. They declare that Silvia's mitochondrial DNA does not match that in the statue as taken by the lab in Bologna. Remember, the Bologna lab did the single-cell analysis in which we could safely exclude the risk of touch DNA contaminating the sample. And while that test could not extract nuclear DNA, it did get mitochondrial DNA. And now we know it wasn't Silvia's.

We can finally say that this woman who kissed and touched her statue and has her DNA all over it, has not fraudulently put her own blood on it. She is in the clear.

★

A New Phase

With me, the doctors were right. There is no miracle cure.

Ron has just visited me here on what I imagine will be my deathbed. He's still going. He's unstoppable. He's promised that we're on the cusp of something big with the mitochondria. That it is there in those genes that follow the maternal line that we will be able to link our samples together with perhaps the Sudarium, and the Shroud of Turin.

Can you imagine that?

If the maternal DNA from the Buenos Aires host matches that from Silvia's statue, or the Miracle of Mexico, or the Shroud! Perhaps some of them are fake. But we only have to link two of them to make that mind-blowing link, that connection that would rock the world. We'll have the blood of Jesus, the mitochondria of Mary.

To find out where it goes, we'll have to wait for Ron's next book, with the working title *More Reasons to Believe*. I'll help him if I can, wherever I am, even if it means he's going to scoop me on the biggest story of all. The only one that matters.

So it goes.

Death awaits. I am thankful. I was blessed with a good life in which I had the privilege to witness some extraordinary things. I hope I have made amends for my sins. I am at peace.

Afterword

Edited extract from the eulogy for Mike Willesee by Father Mark Withoos

Since he decided to take on God's business, it was Mike who combined journalistic skills together with the human sciences, to show that belief in the Eucharist was inherently reasonable. Mike began touring the country talking about his newfound belief that the bread and wine of the Mass truly becomes the body, blood, soul and divinity of Our Lord.

One non-believer approached him at the end of one of his talks and said, 'Well, if this is all true, why doesn't He just show Himself?'

In his usual dry style, Mike said, 'He tried that once.'

It was at one of those talks, in Mike's hometown of Perth no less, that a very important side deal was consummated. Since Mike's return to the Catholic faith he had been praying for his father and mother to come back to the Church and to know and believe what Mike knew to be true. Mike was praying and, of course, God was listening. Mike wanted particularly to give his talk in Perth because there should have been two special people in the audience.

Senator Don Willesee had recently returned to the faith of

his youth after 54 years away. The Senator said that his return had started with one Hail Mary. Over 5000 people turned up for Mike's talk on the Eucharist, the Catholic Mass. The special guests should have been Don and Gwen, coming to hear their son Michael speak, not realising that they were just about to complete the best deal that Mike and Don had ever done.

Before the talk, however, Don suffered a stroke and travel was out of the question.

For Mike, as ever, the show had to go on. Mike went right on to give his talk — he could not leave the thousands who had come to listen — and afterwards, he stayed behind for the hundreds who wanted to talk and ask questions about the faith, and about Mike Willesee. Mike stayed and spoke to every last person. That's just what he did.

Senator Don Willesee received all the sacraments before he died, which was I believe some three days later. The original dealmaker, Senator Don Willesee, completed the deal. Mike was home, back in the faith, but God, who can never be outdone in generosity, wanted it all. Don Willesee was home too.

Michael Willesee was no plaster-cast saint and I'm not here to canonise him. I'm here, rather, to ask you what Mike wants of you now: to pray to God for his eternal soul. God hears prayers. Mike is a testimony to that.

Of course, in a way, Mike is doing the ultimate Willesee deal right now. He has you here for his funeral, he is in need, and he can offer you something hidden on his part, but he wants your part of the deal to be prayers said to help get him to his eternal reward.

If what I am saying to you is true, then there is a sublime beauty to this request. Mike knew too that when you start praying to God, your own soul is also a beneficiary. So while he is asking for your prayers, Mike is also asking that you gain, and come to know God as he did so you can be enriched, and hopefully glorified, by the experience.

ALSO BY MIKE WILLESEE

Memoirs

After thousands of stories, a legend finally tells his own.

Mike Willesee has been Australia's most revered television journalist for over fifty years. And behind the lens, a businessman, powerbroker, trailblazer and enduring enigma.

Son of a minister in the Whitlam cabinet, Willesee was a football star before finding fame as a crusading journalist, and Vietnam War correspondent, for *This Day Tonight* and *Four Corners*. Later, as creator of *A Current Affair*, his interviews became news in themselves, attracting blockbuster ratings, wielding huge political power and transforming him into an icon.

In life, Willesee was a husband and father of six. He made a fortune in radio and television then lost it saving the Sydney Swans and battling his demons.

After a live on-air interview with gunmen secured the release of two children being held hostage, Willesee left *ACA*. He made acclaimed documentaries on subjects as diverse as stigmata and ancient tribes. He survived a plane crash, found God and fought cancer. But he never stopped seeking truth.

Memoirs is that truth – the extraordinary story of Mike Willesee's epic life.

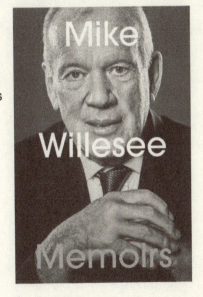